CRIME SCENE INVESTIGATIONS

CRIME SCENE

INVESTIGATIONS

UNDERSTANDING CANADIAN LAW

DANIEL J. BAUM

DUNDURN
TORONTO

Editor: Michael Melgaard
Design: Laura Boyle
Cover Design: Carmen Giraudy
Printer: Webcom

Library and Archives Canada Cataloguing in Publication

Baum, Daniel Jay, 1934-, author
Crime scene investigations : understanding Canadian law / Daniel J. Baum.

Includes index.
Issued in print and electronic formats.
ISBN 978-1-4597-2813-4 (pbk.).--ISBN 978-1-4597-2814-1 (pdf).-- ISBN 978-1-4597-2815-8 (epub)

1. Crime scene searches--Canada. 2. Police--Canada. 3. Criminal law--Canada. I. Title.

KE9265.B39 2015   345.71'052   C2014-907106-X
KF9620.ZA2B39 2015   C2014-907107-8

1 2 3 4 5   19   18 17 16   15

Conseil des Arts du Canada   Canada Council for the Arts

ONTARIO ARTS COUNCIL
CONSEIL DES ARTS DE L'ONTARIO
an Ontario government agency
un organisme du gouvernement de l'Ontario

We acknowledge the support of the **Canada Council for the Arts** and the **Ontario Arts Council** for our publishing program. We also acknowledge the financial support of the **Government of Canada** through the **Canada Book Fund** and **Livres Canada Books**, and the **Government of Ontario** through the Ontario Book Publishing Tax Credit and the **Ontario Media Development Corporation**.

Care has been taken to trace the ownership of copyright material used in this book. The author and the publisher welcome any information enabling them to rectify any references or credits in subsequent editions.
J. Kirk Howard, President

The publisher is not responsible for websites or their content unless they are owned by the publisher.
Printed and bound in Canada.

Visit us at

Dundurn.com | *@dundurnpress* | *Facebook.com/dundurnpress* | *Pinterest.com/dundurnpress*

Dundurn
3 Church Street, Suite 500
Toronto, Ontario, Canada
M5E 1M2

In memory of Norman

CONTENTS

ACKNOWLEDGEMENTS

First, I would like to acknowledge the Supreme Court of Canada. Over the decades, the membership of this nine-person Court has altered through retirement (mandatory at age seventy-five) or death. Increasingly, the Court has tried to hand down judgments that come ever closer to being decisions that can be read, understood, and discussed by those who want to be informed about the structure of our law, of our government, and more importantly, of our society's values. So, I thank — most profusely — the Supreme Court of Canada.

A second link in the chain between the law and the people is the media. It is possible, of course, in our highly computerized society to read the decisions of the Supreme Court of Canada online, but that can be an arduous process. On occasion, magazines such as *Maclean's* feature a particular subject for investigative reporting in which the Supreme Court of Canada's judgments (such as those relating to tobacco) may form a part. Newspapers such as the *Toronto Star* may select a story reflecting a matter of social concern, such as bullying. And, on a daily basis, radio or television may report on such stories.

The net effect of media reporting, at best, ranges from episodic to minimal. Perhaps the one constant to which we frequently refer in this series is the informed editorials in Canada's national newspaper, the *Globe and Mail*. Without hesitating, the *Globe and Mail* granted the right to reprint editorials (and there were many) on Supreme Court of Canada decisions. The approach of the *Globe and Mail* seems to be: Let the public be made aware. I thank them for their generosity and for maintaining consistently high standards.

Ordinarily, I would say that I take full responsibility for the contents of this book. Hopefully, however, the contents do not reflect my judgments but those of the Supreme Court of Canada. My task, as I saw it, was to discuss those judgments in a non-judgmental and accessible way.

INTRODUCTION

A police officer walking a beat or driving a patrol car may be a reassuring sight, giving a sense of security to onlookers. Police presence alone may serve to prevent crime. Yet, crime does occur. This book focuses on crime scene investigations (CSI) — police searches for evidence that can lead to the identity of the wrongdoer and his/her apprehension, trial, and conviction.

The first job of investigating officers is to get the facts and to determine whether charges will be laid and prosecution will follow. The badge and the uniform — both signs of authority — do not give police unlimited power to demand information by way of detention or seizing possible evidence. The Charter of Rights and Freedoms, along with statutes and police regulations, places conditions on how police may go about crime scene investigations

It is the intersect of crime scene investigations and individual rights that is the focus of much of this book.

Police operate under rules which, if allegedly broken, often are investigated by the police themselves. But, there is another kind of review of police action. If the Crown attempts to use tarnished evidence, a court can pass on the matter and, under the Charter, a judge has a wide discretion in determining whether such evidence can be used at trial.

At what point must police inform persons under detention of a right to counsel, and whether a lawyer must be present during police interrogation? This is the subject of Chapter 1.

In Chapter 2 we see an attempt by police to search personal home computers for evidence of child pornography. Such searches, however, may go beyond any evidence of child pornography. How can police know where to look inside the computer? How far can police go in probing the life of an individual and his/her family through inspection of a personal computer?

Proof of crime may lie beyond police questioning or examination of a suspect's personal computer. Proof may come from such mundane objects as garbage which, by definition, is intended to be discarded. On what basis, then, may an individual assert a "privilege" of ownership and privacy against a police garbage search? To the police, however, such refuse may tell a story. It may disclose a lifestyle; it may even point to evidence of crime, such as the use of prohibited drugs.

In addition, there are searches that have the appearance of not being searches at all. Suppose police suspect a home is being used as a "grow-op" — a place for the unlawful cultivation of marijuana. One way to get evidence that, in turn, might be used to justify a search warrant is a plane "fly-over" with heat sensors — police can establish whether an inordinate amount of heat generated by electricity is being used at the suspected house. That excess heat could serve to aid in the cultivation of marijuana plants. Such a fly-over is a search, but is it subject to legal limits?

We return to the police on patrol. Their training and everyday experience gives them a sense of their "turf." Here we come to the police "pat-down," an intersect between police investigation and individual privacy rights. Consider an individual walking on a sidewalk. On the face of it, she has done no wrong. However, the area is one designated by police as "high crime." Two police officers doing their regular beat stop the walker and proceed to do a patdown. An officer brushes the outside of the walker's clothing and finds a "bulge." She reaches inside to find that the bulge is a packet containing cocaine. An arrest is made, and charges are laid. The question: Was the search legal? This is the subject of Chapter 3.

In crime scene investigations, police can make mistakes that can be costly and otherwise hurtful to the persons investigated. Sometimes, they reach what may appear to be a dead end in their investigations. In Chapters 4 and 5 we discuss other methods used by police in their search for the facts. Topics range from hypnosis to DNA testing.

Police investigations may be like links in a chain, where one link seems to lead to another, forging a chain that leads to charges and conviction of a person who later is found to be innocent. And, there are times when police investigations are conducted negligently — even knowingly so. Are there any remedies for such police and Crown action? Will the victim be inhibited from bringing forward such action? This is the subject of Chapter 6.

WHO ARE THE JUDGES?

A few words must be said about the judges (or justices, as Supreme Court of Canada judges are called). Who are they? How are they chosen? How do they go about coming to decisions? The answer to these questions may help us better understand the decisions that we will be examining.

In 1989 Beverley McLachlin, then chief justice of British Columbia, received a telephone call from the prime minister of Canada. He asked if she would consider a new position: that of a justice of the Supreme Court of Canada.

It was within the power of the prime minister, accepted by his Cabinet, to offer the position. The appointment of a justice of the Supreme Court of Canada did not have to go through parliamentary committee or parliamentary consent, as such — a process enormously different from that of the United States, where the president nominates and the Senate, following hearing, either gives the nomination a stamp of approval or rejection. (If the Senate rejects, then the candidacy of that person comes to an end.)

Justice McLachlin thanked the prime minister, accepted his offer, and became a justice of the Supreme Court of Canada. On January 7, 2000, the prime minister offered Justice McLachlin the position of chief justice of the Supreme Court, and she accepted.

There are nine justices who make up the Supreme Court of Canada. The conditions for their appointment are few, but they are important. They are appointed through the prime minister and the Governor in Council. In this regard, the "pool" for appointment by law is comprised of superior court judges or barristers with at least ten years in practice in a province or territory.

Once named to the Supreme Court, a justice cannot be removed from office so long as the justice carries out her/his duties in accordance with the law. But, at the age of seventy-five, there is forced retirement. (However, many retired justices are called back to serve in appointments such as chairing special commissions.) A serving justice can only be removed from office for bad conduct or incapacity (such as illness).

By law, the prime minister is required to appoint three justices from Quebec. By tradition, the prime minister also appoints three justices from Ontario, two from the West, and one from Atlantic Canada.

How the prime minister goes about selecting a justice for the Supreme Court, given the broad limits described, is for the prime minister to determine. In 2012 Prime Minister Stephen Harper set new guidelines. He named a panel of five members of the House of Commons: three Conservatives (the prime minister's governing party), one New Democrat, and one Liberal. Their task was to review a list of qualified candidates put forward by the federal justice minister in consultation with the prime minister, the chief justice of the Supreme Court of Canada, the chief justice of Quebec (where the next justice was to be selected), the Attorney General of Quebec, and provincial and territorial bar associations (as well as public suggestions).

The panel was instructed to submit a list of three recommended candidates — unranked — to the prime minister and he would select one from that list. A public hearing before a special parliamentary committee would be held before the prime minister finalized the appointment.

The first justice selected through the process described above was Richard Wagner, who was a long-time trial lawyer before becoming a justice of the Quebec Court of Appeal. In an interview with the *Globe and Mail*, Justice Wagner said: "I might surprise you, but I liked the [hearing] process. There is nothing to hide. I think a judge should follow the directions of society, and that means to explain to citizens what we do, how we do it and why we do it. I think it's fair and it's reasonable."

A central concern, said Justice Wagner, is ensuring access to the justice system for all Canadians.

SOME FACTS

On the whole, it can be said that justices of the Supreme Court of Canada historically do not like to talk about themselves. But, there are some facts that may give rise to questions going to the makeup of the Court:

- There have been no persons "of colour" appointed to the Supreme Court of Canada.
- There have been no persons from among the "first peoples" (First Nations, Métis, and Inuit) appointed to the Supreme Court of Canada.

The fact is that white men, drawn from an elite part of the legal profession, constituted the "pool" from which justices of the Supreme Court of Canada were drawn — at least until 1982. In that year — at the time the Charter of Rights and Freedoms, an important part of the Constitution of Canada, came into effect — the prime minister named the first woman to the Supreme Court: Bertha Wilson. She had immigrated to Canada with her husband John, a Presbyterian minister in Scotland, in 1949.

Justice Wilson had received an M.A. in philosophy at the

University of Aberdeen. Once in Canada, she applied for admission to the law program at Dalhousie University in Halifax. She recalled an interview with the dean of the law school, and chuckled about it later. The dean advised her to "go home and take up crocheting." She didn't. She entered the Dalhousie law program in 1955 and was called to the Nova Scotia Bar after graduation.

In 1959 Justice Wilson moved to Toronto where she found employment with a leading law firm and later became head of research for that firm. Her job consisted in no small measure in writing opinions for members of the firm — a task that went a long way toward preparing her for work as a judge.

Justice Wilson received an invitation in 1979 to sit as a judge on the Ontario Court of Appeal. Her immediate response was surprise — and then laughter when, as a judge whose opinions reflected women's rights, she said: "I'll have to talk it over with my husband." She accepted the position on the Court of Appeal and served there until her appointment to the Supreme Court of Canada.

Justice Wilson was a Supreme Court justice from 1982 to 1991, retiring at the age of sixty-eight. There, she had an important role in interpreting the then newly-established Charter of Rights and Freedoms, including decisions relating to a woman's right to abortion (*The Queen v. Morgentaler* [1988] 1 *Supreme Court of Canada Reports* 30) and a spouse's right to claim self-defence to murder based on physical abuse by her/his spouse (called in law the battered wife syndrome) (*The Queen v. Lavallée* [1990] 1 *Supreme Court of Canada Reports* 852).

Since the appointment of Justice Wilson, a number of women have served as justices of the Supreme Court of Canada. In 2012, after serving as a justice for what she called ten "intense" years, Justice Marie Deschamps of Quebec resigned at the age of fifty-nine. (At that time, there were four women sitting as justices.) In an interview with CBC News a week after her resignation, Justice Deschamps was asked about "gender balance" on the Court. She answered, "I think every court should aim for half and half.... It's important that [the Court] is balanced.... I hope that the government will maintain at least four women on the Court. Whether the next candidate is a woman or it's the one that follows it will be for the government to decide."

In fact, the prime minister named Justice Richard Wagner of Quebec to the Court, thus lowering the number of women justices (at least for the time) to three.

It should be noted that the chief justice at the time of Justice Deschamps's resignation was Beverley McLachlin (*CBC.ca*, August 15, 2012).

HOW ARE JUDGES TO DECIDE?

May emotion play a role in decision-making? For us, in reviewing decisions of the Supreme Court of Canada (or the decisions of any court, for that matter), an important question is whether justices can decide a case largely on the facts and the law as given. Can they remove (or largely isolate) any individual bias?

There are two parts to the answer — at least as applied to the Supreme Court of Canada:

1. No single justice decides a case. If the Court sits as a panel, there usually are seven justices who meet, discuss, and work toward an opinion which the chief justice usually assigns to a specific justice. If there is disagreement that cannot be otherwise resolved, then the way is open to a written dissent or a concurring opinion. (Often the justices are able to work out their disagreement to form a majority or a unanimous opinion.)

2. A case may be one that summons enormous emotion. Such was the case of Robert Latimer, a Saskatchewan farmer charged and convicted in the "mercy" killing of his disabled daughter. Twice the case went on appeal to the Supreme

Court of Canada. The second time, the appeal was from a judgment of the Saskatchewan Court of Appeal that had increased a sentence of one year to ten years.

In a decision by the Court as a whole in the Latimer case — not one attributed to any particular justice — the Supreme Court of Canada affirmed the judgment. The role of emotion in coming to decision was lessened.

Justice Ian Binnie, on his retirement after serving fourteen years on the Court, commented on the Latimer case in an extensive interview with Kirk Makin of the *Globe and Mail*:

> The Robert Latimer case was a hugely controversial case, but to me, the legal outcome was straightforward. You can't have people making their own judgments as to whether their child should live or die.
>
> In saying that, I make no moral judgment about what Latimer did. I accept his word that he did it because he thought it was best for his daughter.
>
> But the legal decision wasn't his to make. But the law is clear. When you talk about judges applying the law and not making it up, if the Criminal Code is clear about the penalty that follows from the crime of homicide, then that is the penalty that follows. You can't apply the law differently from case to case depending on a judge's personal view of whether a constitutional exemption is warranted.
>
> So, there is no necessary [relation] between how much you agonize over a decision and what the moral implications or the controversy is outside the courtroom. My only function in that case is the right legal result. In that case the legal result

was clear. My personal views of whether it was a good outcome or a bad outcome were irrelevant (*Globe and Mail*, September 23, 2011).

REFERENCES AND FURTHER READING

Fitzpatrick, Meagan. "Supreme Court Should Have Four Women Says Retiring Justice," *CBC.ca*, August 15, 2012.

Makin, Kirk. "Justice Ian Binnie's Exit Interview." *Globe and Mail*, September 23, 2011.

_____. "Supreme Court Judge Warns of 'Dangerous' Flaws in the System." *Globe and Mail*, December 12, 2012.

1

CHAPTER 1

POLICE QUESTIONING: MUST A LAWYER BE PRESENT?

Science in crime detection dates back more than two centuries. It includes photography, fingerprinting, and blood samples. Perhaps, however, no technique is more important to effective investigation than police finding and questioning witnesses who, in violent crimes such as murders, often become suspects.

In this chapter we will explore how police, in conducting a criminal investigation, must do so in ways that satisfy the fundamental rights of Canadians — with special reference to the Charter of Rights and Freedoms. (The Charter is part of the Constitution of Canada and, as such, is the highest law of the land. The final interpretation as to the meaning of the Charter — subject to a quite limited exception called the notwithstanding clause — is that given by the Supreme Court of Canada.)

The principal case in this chapter is *The Queen v. Sinclair*, 2010 *Supreme Court of Canada Reports* 35. It deals with police questioning of a murder suspect and that person's right to consult a lawyer of his choice before any interrogation.

Sinclair was arrested in British Columbia and charged with second degree murder. He was subject to "custodial questioning" by police following that arrest. (Two companion cases were also decided by the Supreme Court. They will be presented as "You Be the Judge" exercises.)

Among the questions raised in this chapter are:

- At what point does an arrested person have a right to the advice of a lawyer (counsel)?
- What are an individual's rights in terms of having a lawyer of his/her choice?
- Does the right to counsel include the opportunity to have the arrested person's lawyer present at every stage of questioning?
- Can such contact be limited to one telephone call?
- When, if at all, must police renew the right to counsel if the arrested person initially refused the offer?
- If the right to counsel is denied, does it follow that evidence unlawfully obtained will be excluded from trial?

WHO ARE LAW ENFORCEMENT OFFICERS?

Much police work does not relate to crime but to the maintenance of order and safety. For example, a large number of police within any department have little responsibility, as such, over serious crimes (felonies). Traffic officers — those charged with helping to maintain safety on streets and highways — are only incidentally involved with the criminal law, such as when there is an arrest for excessive speeding, impaired driving, or serious injury through driver negligence.

Most people thought of as law enforcement officers in fact are not police. In 2006 there were about 102,000 private security personnel in Canada, compared to 68,000 police officers. This means that there were about three private security personnel for every two regular police officers. Security guards made up 90 percent of private security personnel.

Between 2001 and 2006 private security forces in Canada grew by 15 percent. In that same period, regular police forces increased by 3 percent.

Private officers may be in uniform. They may be prohibited from carrying restraints such as handcuffs, mace, or batons. Some officers, such as those transporting valuable goods, may be licensed to carry weapons. On demand, they may be required to produce identification. Most private law enforcement officers are employed by companies such as those managing or constructing buildings or shopping malls.

Private officers are subject to government licensing. And, over the years, the licensing process has become more demanding — though not nearly as stringent as it is in those special schools established for those seeking police jobs.

However, some of these private security organizations seem almost like regular police forces. For example, in Canada there is an organization nearly a century old called the Commissionaires. It is a private security firm that originally hired largely retired military personnel, but now includes former police officers and others. Its contracts are largely, though not exclusively, with government. Its employees can be found as guards at military installations in the company's own unique uniforms. Their employer is not the government but the Commissionaires. They wear insignia of rank and follow a military-type structure.

THE POWER OF PRIVATE SECURITY GUARDS

Private security officers have the power to protect property and, should they witness any crime, to make a "citizen's arrest." If there is a home break-in — in a gated community, for example — the likelihood is that the incident is reported to the police. (If goods are stolen and they are insured, then the insurance company probably will require a police report of the incident as a condition for collecting on the insurance policy.)

THE POWER OF POLICE

For the most part, we understand that police carry a badge and are trained and employed by government. They are subject to government regulation in terms of how they are to respond to reported crimes. And, their behaviour is subject to military-style discipline, including the possibility of discharge for serious violation of police rules.

Often police are in uniform and drive specially marked vehicles. (Sometimes, however, they are not in uniform. "Detectives" frequently are in "plain clothes.") It is fair to say that police, as they are employed by government, are set up along military lines. Police have the power, in law, to arrest those within their jurisdiction on a showing of probable cause, and to lay charges which the Crown may prosecute in the criminal courts.

WHY THE DIFFERENCE?

As a practical matter, what is the difference between a "regular" police officer and a private security guard? A regular police officer is an employee of government and she/he is licensed by government. It follows that her/his actions can be seen as the actions of government. For the most part, the discussion in this chapter focusses on regular police.

The Charter of Rights and Freedoms applies to regular police officers, though not to private security guards. And the Charter, as noted, is part of the Constitution of Canada which sets standards that the police must observe in their dealing with individuals. These include affording rights under section 10, including the obligation to be informed "promptly of the reasons for arrest or detention," the right to obtain and instruct a lawyer, and the right to have the validity of such detention determined by a court of law.

Section 32 of the Charter provides that it: "(1)(a) applies to the Parliament and government of Canada in respect of all matters within the authority of Parliament including all matters relating to the Yukon Territory and Northwest Territories; and (b) to the legislature and government of each province in respect of all matters within the authority of the legislature of each province."

THE SINCLAIR CASE: THE FACTS

As noted, the Sinclair case will be the main judgment for discussion relating to adults. There the Court divided, with the majority ruling that it was enough for the police to have given a murder suspect the opportunity for a brief phone call to his lawyer. In a 5–4 decision, Chief Justice McLachlin and Justice Louise Charron wrote the majority opinion in which Justices Deschamps, Marshall Rothstein, and Thomas Cromwell concurred. Justice Binnie wrote a dissenting opinion, and Justices Louis LeBel and Morris Fish, joined by Justice Rosalie Abella, wrote another dissent.

The facts, as in most cases, are important in order to recognize the issues and to understand the decision reached — both as to majority, concurring, and dissenting opinions. (One never knows when a differently constituted Court may look at a dissent and use it to read more narrowly the majority opinion. Supreme Court justices must retire at age seventy-five. The result is that the Court composition is always in a state of change.)

Sinclair was charged with second degree murder in the November 21, 2002 killing of Gary Grice, and ultimately was convicted by a jury of the lesser offence of manslaughter. The events that concern us on this appeal took place following Sinclair's arrest early in the morning of Saturday, December 14, 2002, by members of the RCMP detachment in Vernon, British Columbia.

It was then that RCMP officers told Sinclair that he was being arrested for the killing of Grice, that he had the right to retain and instruct counsel without delay, that he could call any lawyer he wanted, and that a Legal Aid lawyer would be available free of charge. When asked whether he wanted to call a lawyer, Sinclair responded: "Not right this second." He was then taken to the RCMP detachment, with assurances that he would have another opportunity to contact counsel once he got there.

After booking (being formally charged by police), Sinclair was again asked whether he wanted to exercise his right to counsel. This time he told the officer, Corporal Leibel, that he wanted to speak with a lawyer named Victor S. Janicki, whom he had once retained to defend him on an unrelated charge. The police placed the call and Sinclair spoke with Janicki by phone in a private room for about three minutes. Corporal Leibel asked Sinclair whether he was satisfied with the call, and Sinclair answered: "Yeah, he's taking my case."

About three hours later, Corporal Leibel called Janicki to find out if he was coming to the police station to meet with Sinclair. Janicki said no because he did not yet have a Legal Aid retainer, but he asked to speak with Sinclair again by phone. Another three minute phone call in a private room with Sinclair followed. And, again, Sinclair told Corporal Leibel that he was satisfied with the call.

Later that day, Sinclair was interviewed for about five hours by Sergeant Skrine, a police officer with training as an interrogator. Before the interview began, Sergeant Skrine confirmed with Sinclair that he had been advised of and had exercised his right to counsel. The officer also warned Sinclair that he did not have to say anything and informed him that the interview was being recorded and could be used in court.

Then, as Skrine began to ask Sinclair harmless questions about his background and upbringing, Sinclair stated that he had nothing to say "until my lawyer's around and he tells me what's goin' on and stuff, like [that]...." Sergeant Skrine responded: "Fair enough." He assured Sinclair that he indeed had the right not to speak.

Sergeant Skrine also said that, as he understood the law in Canada, Sinclair had the right to consult his lawyer but that he did not have the right to have the lawyer present during questioning. Sinclair appeared to accept this, and the interview continued with Sergeant Skrine attempting to build trust with Mr. Sinclair while getting some preliminary information.

A short time later, Sinclair again said he was uncomfortable being interviewed in the absence of his lawyer. Sergeant Skrine replied that Sinclair had the right to choose whether to talk or not, but that his right to counsel had already been satisfied by the earlier telephone calls. This explanation seemed to satisfy Sinclair for the time being, and the questioning continued.

That questioning then shifted to the crime itself. Sergeant Skrine focused on the crime scene. He told Sinclair for the first time that police knew it was Grice's blood on the carpet in his hotel room. Sinclair stated: "Well I choose to say nothing at the moment." Sergeant Skrine responded "Fair enough," and he continued to reveal details about the investigation.

Bear in mind that this was ongoing questioning in a confined space — in a small room with no windows — and, on the whole, with no breaks from the questioning.

Shortly after, Sinclair repeated that he was "not talking right now" and that he wanted to speak to his lawyer about "all this." Sergeant Skrine told him that it was his decision whether to speak or not.

Still, the interview continued in this manner for some time. Four or five times, Sinclair said he wanted to speak with his lawyer and that he intended to remain silent on matters touching on the murder. Each time, Sergeant Skrine emphasized that it was Sinclair's choice to make.

On one of these occasions, Sinclair expressed uncertainty about what he should do. He said: "Just don't know what to do right now. And that's why I say I wanna wait and think and muddle things through my mind and talk to my lawyer and talk to people.... I know you're tryin' to do your job. And I do think you're doin' a good job, it's just I just don't know what to say at the moment."

Sergeant Skrine began to get the kind of answers he was looking for. Sinclair commented "You already knew all the answers before you even brought me into the room," and he began to describe what had happened between him and Grice.

According to Sinclair, the two men had been drinking liquor and Grice had been using cocaine in Sinclair's hotel room. They were both intoxicated. At one point Grice approached Sinclair holding a knife. Sinclair thought that Grice wanted money for another fix and reacted by hitting him over the head with a frying pan. A struggle ensued, and Sinclair ended up stabbing Grice several times and slitting his throat. He disposed of the body and the bloodied bedding in a dumpster.

Later, the police placed Mr. Sinclair in a cell with an undercover officer who was aware that Sinclair had been under lengthy questioning. Sinclair said to him: "They've got me, the body, the sheets, the blood, the fibres on the carpet, witnesses. I'm going away for a long time but I feel relieved." He explained that he would not have to keep looking over his shoulder for the police.

Sinclair also accompanied the police to where Grice had been killed, and he participated in a re-enactment.

THE SINCLAIR CASE: THE DECISION

The Charter rights raised in the Sinclair case are:

- Everyone has the right on arrest or detention to retain and instruct counsel without delay and to be informed of that right (section 10(b)).
- Any person charged with an offence has the right not to be compelled to be a witness in proceedings against himself/herself in respect of the offence (section 7).
- Any confession with respect to any charged offence must be informed and voluntary.

THE MAJORITY DECISION

Chief Justice McLachlin and Justice Charron, as noted, wrote the majority opinion in which Justices Deschamps, Rothstein, and Cromwell concurred, thus making the Court judgment a 5–4 decision. Their primary focus was on section 10(b) of the Charter. If that section could be read as guaranteeing a right to counsel even during police interrogation, that would have been the end of the matter. Sinclair would have won the case. Police denial of the right to his counsel to sit in on the interrogation of Sinclair would have been ruled unconstitutional because it would have violated the Charter.

However, the Court majority did not give section 10(b) that reading. Rather, the majority stated that a "deeper purposive analysis is required." Essentially, the arrested person has a decision to make in the exercise of his/her section 10(b) right to counsel — whether to co-operate with police interrogation, or not. The Court majority stated:

> The purpose of the right to counsel is to allow the detainee not only to be informed of his rights and obligations under the law, but equally if not more important, to obtain advice as to how to exercise those rights.... The emphasis, therefore, is on assuring that the detainee's decision to cooperate with the investigation or decline to do so is free and informed. Section 10(b) does not guarantee that the detainee's decision is wise; nor does it guard against subjective factors that may influence the decision. Its purpose is simply to give detainees the opportunity to access legal advice relevant to that choice.
>
> Section 10(b) fulfills its purpose in two ways. First, it requires that the detainee be advised of his right to counsel. This is called the informational component. Second, it requires that the detainee be given an opportunity to exercise his

right to consult counsel. This is called the implementational component. Failure to comply with either of these components frustrates the purpose of section 10(b) and results in a breach of the detainee's rights.... Implied in the second component is a duty on the police to hold off questioning until the detainee has had a reasonable opportunity to consult counsel.

RE-CONSULT COUNSEL

In effect, the majority opinion accepted the right of Sinclair to consult counsel in order to understand his rights and what he had to do to affect them. But, in the exercise of these rights, the majority opinion emphasized the need for balance. This seemed to mean that the right to retain and instruct counsel had to be done in the context of allowing police to pursue their legitimate investigative goals. The Court majority stated:

> These purposes can be achieved by the right to re-consult counsel where developments make this necessary.... They do not demand the continued presence of counsel throughout the interview process....
>
> The scope of s. 10(b) of the Charter must be defined by reference to its language; the right to silence; the common law confessions rule [section 7]; and the public interest in effective law enforcement in the Canadian context.... We conclude that s. 10(b) should not be interpreted as conferring a constitutional right to have a lawyer present throughout a police interview. *There is of course nothing to prevent counsel from being present at an interrogation where all sides consent.... The police*

remain free to facilitate such an arrangement if they so choose, and the detainee may wish to make counsel's presence a precondition of giving a statement [emphasis added].

Yet, what are some of the conditions which would require police to give the arrested person the right to re-consult counsel? The Court majority stated:

> Sometimes developments occur which require a second consultation in order to allow the accused to get the advice he needs to exercise his right to choose in the new situation.
>
> The general idea that underlies the cases where the Court has upheld a second right to consult with counsel is that changed circumstances suggest that reconsultation is necessary in order for the detainee to have the information relevant to choosing whether to cooperate with the police investigation or not. The concern is that in the new or newly revealed circumstances, the initial advice may no longer be adequate.

The Court majority then gave situations when the opportunity to re-consult counsel may be required. The list was not intended to be complete:

> (1) New Procedures Involving the Detainee
> The initial advice of legal counsel will be geared to the expectation that the police will seek to question the detainee. Non-routine procedures, like participation in a line-up or submitting to a polygraph, will not generally fall within the expectation of the advising lawyer at the time of

the initial consultation. It follows that to meet the purpose of section 10(b) to give the detainee the information needed to make a meaningful choice about whether to cooperate in these new procedures, further advice from counsel is necessary.

(2) Change in Jeopardy

Section 10(a) of the Charter requires police to give reasons for detention. And, it is in this context that the individual seeks counsel. If the investigation takes a new and more serious turn as events unfold, that advice may no longer be adequate. To meet the purpose of s. 10(b), the detainee must be given a further opportunity to consult with counsel and obtain advice on the new situation.

(3) Reason to Question the Detainee's Understanding of his Section 10(b) Right

It may be that the arrested person did not understand her/his right to counsel. If the police are (or reasonably should have been) aware of this, there is a duty to again give that person the right to seek counsel. So, too, if police in their questioning of the arrested person 'undermine' the advice counsel has given, there may be a further need to all for re-consultation.

The Court majority continued: "The change of circumstances, the cases suggest, must be objectively observable in order to trigger re-consultation. It is not enough for the accused to assert, after the fact, confusion or the need for help."

There must be, said the Court majority, "objective indicators that renewed legal consultation was required to permit him to make a meaningful choice as to whether to co-operate with the police investigation or refuse to do so."

In his dissent in the Sinclair case, Justice Binnie would have expanded the category to include all situations where the detainee reasonably requests re-consultation in the course of a custodial interview. He then set out a non-exhaustive list of factors which may provide reasonable grounds for a further consultation for the guidance of police and reviewing courts.

The Court majority stated:

> We conclude that the principles and case-law do not support the view that a request, without more, is sufficient to re-trigger the section 10(b) right to counsel.... What is required is a change in circumstances that suggests that the choice faced by the accused has been significantly altered, requiring further advice on the new situation, in order to fulfill the purpose of section 10(b) of providing the accused with legal advice relevant to the choice of whether to cooperate with the police investigation or not. Police tactics short of such a change may result in the Crown being unable to prove beyond a reasonable doubt that a subsequent statement was voluntary, rendering it inadmissible. But it does not follow that the procedural rights granted by s. 10(b) have been breached.

DUTY ON THE DETAINEE

In *The Queen v. Sinclair*, the Court majority made it clear that Sinclair had responsibilities to make effective his section 10(b) rights. He had to assert his Charter rights, or he could "waive" those rights. The Court majority stated:

The police obligations flowing from section 10(b) are not absolute. Unless a detainee [Sinclair] invokes the right and is reasonably diligent in exercising it, the correlative duties on the police to provide a reasonable opportunity and to refrain from eliciting evidence will either not arise in the first place or will be suspended.

Once informed of his right to consult counsel, the detainee may waive the right, deciding not to avail himself of the opportunity to consult that has been provided. The right to choose whether to cooperate with the police, the basic purpose of section 10(b) has been respected in the event of a valid waiver, and there is consequently no breach.

A RIGHT TO SILENCE

Is the right to be silent the same as the right to counsel within the meaning of section 10(b) of the Charter?

To the Court majority in the Sinclair case, the right to retain and consult counsel is related to, but stands independently of, the right to be silent under section 7 of the Charter. The Court majority said:

The section 10(b) right to consult and retain counsel and to be advised of that right supports the broader section 7 right to silence. However, it is not to be confused with the right to silence.

An important purpose of legal advice is to inform the accused about his right to choose whether to co-operate with the police investigation and how to exercise it. Section 10(b) is a specific right directed at one aspect of protecting the right to silence — the opportunity to secure legal assistance [emphasis added].

A given case may raise both section 10(b) and section 7 issues. Where it is alleged under section 7 and the confessions rule that a statement is involuntary because of denial of the right to consult counsel, the factual underpinning of the two inquiries may overlap.... Yet they remain distinct inquiries. *The fact that the police complied with section 10(b) does not mean that a statement is voluntary under the confessions rule* [that is, a rule as to when and under what circumstances a confession will be deemed voluntary]. Conversely, the fact that a statement is made voluntarily does not rule out breach of s. 10(b). It follows that ... the section 7 right to silence does not resolve the issue on this appeal [emphasis added].

RESTORING POWER BALANCE BETWEEN POLICE AND DETAINEE?

The majority opinion continued:

Mr. Sinclair argues that the purpose of s. 10(b) is broader than this. In his view, accepted by our colleagues LeBel and Fish JJ. [dissenting], the purpose of section 10(b) is to advise the detainee how to deal with police questions. The detainee, it is argued, is in the power of the police. The purpose of section 10(b) is to restore a power-balance between the detainee and the police in the coercive atmosphere of the police investigation. On this view, the purpose of the right is not so much informational as protection [for the detainee].

We cannot accept this view of the purpose of section 10(b). As will be discussed more fully ... this view of section 10(b) goes against 25 years of jurisprudence defining section 10(b) in terms of the right to consult counsel to obtain information and advice immediately upon detention, but not as providing ongoing legal assistance during the course of the interview that follows, regardless of the circumstances.

We conclude that in the context of a custodial interrogation, the purpose of section 10(b) is to support the detainee's right to choose whether to cooperate with the police investigation or not, by giving him access to legal advice on the situation he is facing. This is achieved by requiring that he be informed of the right to consult counsel and, if he so requests, be given an opportunity to consult counsel [emphasis added].

RE-CONSULTATION FOR SINCLAIR?

The Court majority asked whether the facts called for the opportunity for Sinclair to have a re-consultation with his lawyer — or, putting it another way, whether he should have had the chance to rethink co-operation with the police. The Court majority answered this question in the negative, stating:

Mr. Sinclair's jeopardy remained the same throughout; he knew from the outset he was facing a charge of murder. The evidence the police told him about did not change the jeopardy he was facing. The police were not requesting his co-operation in a line-up. And as the Court of Appeal held, the police representations as to the strength of the evidence against him do not, without more, raise the need for further consultation with a lawyer.

The only possibility for Sinclair to obtain re-consultation, said the Court majority — on the facts of the case — was if he were "confused" about his choices, of his right to remain silent. The Court majority stated:

> The sequence of the interview relevant to this line of inquiry begins with Mr. Sinclair's reaction to Sergeant Skrine's statement that the case against him was "absolutely overwhelming."
> To this Mr. Sinclair answered, "I want my lawyer to look through all that." This can be interpreted as a need for legal advice on the actual strength of the case against him....
> Mr. Sinclair continued to ask for legal advice. On one of these occasions, quoted before he expressed uncertainty about what to do, [he stated]: "Just don't know what to do right now. And that's why I say I wanna wait and think and muddle things through my mind and talk to my lawyer and talk to people.... I know you're tryin' to do your job. And I do think you're doin' a good job, it's just *I just don't know what to say at the moment*" [emphasis added].
> Read broadly and in isolation, these passages arguably support the allegation that Mr. Sinclair may have been confused about his rights and how he should exercise them. However, read in context, it is clear that Mr. Sinclair never had any doubt about the choices the law allowed him and, in particular, his constitutional right to remain silent. The police did not denigrate the legal advice he had

received. Rather, they repeatedly confirmed that it was Mr. Sinclair's choice whether or not to speak.

After his confession, and the so-called re-enactment, Mr. Sinclair had an exchange with Sergeant Skrine [the police interrogator] which made clear his awareness of the choice he faced and the fact that it went against the advice of his lawyer.

The Court continued its recitation of the interrogation:

> Sinclair: Lawyer'll probably be mad that I told everything out but it's like whatever....
>
> Skrine: Yeah. Well you know and that's what I said up front. I mean you're given advice, but at the end of the day you make the decision right?
>
> Sinclair: Yeah.
>
> Skrine: It's your decision to make. Um in this country and you know my opinion is you made the right decision right?
>
> Sinclair: *Well now there's closure* [emphasis added].

FINDINGS OF THE TRIAL COURT QUOTED

The majority opinion of the Court quoted the following findings of the trial judge, stating that they confirmed that Mr. Sinclair was never confused about his legal options:

- "I am satisfied by [Mr. Sinclair's] own comments that he understood his right was to remain silent, to choose whether to speak or not. Nobody ever tried to tell him that he did not have that right...."
- "Mr. Sinclair's counsel advised him not to discuss anything important with anybody, advised about some of

the devices the police might use, including a cell plant, and advised not to say anything 'because they lie.'"

- "The police did not make any attempt to denigrate counsel or the advice he had received from counsel. All they did was confirm that ultimately it was Mr. Sinclair's decision as to whether he said anything or not."

- "'I am satisfied that [Mr. Sinclair] is certainly intelligent enough to understand what his situation was and to make his own choices."

- "What, in my opinion, happened in this case is that all of the efforts that Sergeant Skrine made to try and encourage Mr. Sinclair to speak were without avail. Mr. Sinclair stood up to them very well."

- "Ultimately when Mr. Sinclair knew that the body had been found, that is when he decided the game was up and he thought he may as well come clean and he did so, not because anybody offered him anything, because it relieved him of the pressure he was under, the police investigation, not the interview, and as he said himself, the court might look more kindly on him having co-operated and that is why he decided to do the re-enactment as well."

- "After he had made his initial statement, Mr. Sinclair told his cell mate (who was in fact an undercover police officer): 'They've got me, the body, the sheets, the blood, the fibres on the carpet, witnesses. I'm going away for a long time but I feel relieved.'"

The Court majority in *The Queen v. Sinclair* stated: "We conclude that Mr. Sinclair's claim that his s. 10(b) Charter rights were infringed has not been made out."

YOU BE THE JUDGE

THE CASE OF THE REPEATED REQUEST

The case that follows is real. The facts are detailed because they bear upon the issues to be decided and because they have some obvious similarity to the Sinclair case.

THE FACTS

On December 3, 2005, the RCMP arrested Donald Russell McCrimmon at his home in relation to eight assaults against five different women over the past few months. He was alleged to have picked up the women in downtown Chilliwack, British Columbia, driven them to an isolated area, and assaulted them. Two of the women alleged that he had drugged them with what turned out to be chloroform. The offences with which he was charged included assault, sexual assault, assault causing bodily harm, unlawful confinement, and the administration of a noxious substance with intent to cause bodily harm.

At the outset of his arrest, Constable Laurel Mathew advised McCrimmon of the reasons for his arrest, his right to retain and instruct counsel, and his right to remain silent. She told him that he could call any lawyer he wanted, and that he had a right to contact a Legal Aid lawyer through a twenty-four-hour telephone service. McCrimmon stated that he wished to speak to a specific lawyer, a person who had once represented him.

Constable Mathew took McCrimmon to a nearby RCMP detachment where he gave the name of his "preferred"

Vancouver lawyer. Constable Mathew called that lawyer's office but was unable to reach him. However, she left a message on the answering machine. She did not attempt to find the lawyer's home telephone number, nor did McCrimmon ask her to do so. He said to her: "I don't know if I'll hear back from him. Like I said, I only used him once. He's the only guy I know. I've never really dealt with a lawyer before."

Constable Mathew asked McCrimmon if he would like to call a Legal Aid lawyer, to which he replied: "Well, yes, definitely, but I prefer [the lawyer who once represented me]." McCrimmon then spoke privately with Legal Aid's duty counsel for approximately five minutes. At the end of his conversation, he confirmed that he was satisfied with the consultation and that he understood the advice provided by duty counsel.

At 5:15 p.m., Sergeant Allan Proulx, an officer with specialized training in interrogation techniques, took McCrimmon into an interview room outfitted with an audio and video recorder and spoke with him for more than three hours. At the outset of the interview, McCrimmon confirmed having spoken with a Legal Aid lawyer, revealing that he had been advised that he did not have to say anything to the police. Sergeant Proulx affirmed McCrimmon's right to silence, cautioned him that anything he said could be used against him, and commenced the investigative interview.

When the interview began, McCrimmon said he first wanted to speak with his lawyer, though he didn't mind speaking with Sergeant Proulx. Sergeant Proulx again told McCrimmon it was his choice to speak or keep silent, but that his lawyer would not be allowed in the interview room.

Then, for about ten minutes, Sergeant Proulx explained "the incriminatory nature of potential DNA evidence." Again, McCrimmon asked to speak with his lawyer. And, again, Sergeant Proulx refused, stating that McCrimmon had already exercised that right in his conversation with duty counsel — advice with which McCrimmon, at the time, seemed satisfied. McCrimmon did not dispute this but asked to be taken back to his cell. He was not going to answer any more questions. Sergeant Proulx told McCrimmon he did not have to answer questions but that it was his job as a police officer to provide him with the facts.

Sergeant Proulx continued the interview, the purpose of which seemed to be to persuade McCrimmon to discuss the incidents under investigation. He scattered his remarks with references to what the police knew about the incident and referred to witness statements. When pressed for his version of events, McCrimmon emphasized the absence of his lawyer, his sense of feeling "vulnerable without any representation," and his ignorance of "the legal ways."

McCrimmon insisted that he would not speak without his lawyer present. He stated: "My voice will be heard in the end, with my lawyer," and said that he was "adamant about that." Sergeant Proulx affirmed that McCrimmon had the right to exercise his right to silence and that he did not have "to keep repeating it ... to get that."

Sergeant Proulx then carried on with long monologues obviously designed to establish a rapport with McCrimmon and elicit information from him. Later, steering the topic of conversation back to the alleged offences, Sergeant Proulx related more details known to the police, prompting McCrimmon to begin describing his version of the events.

As Sergeant Proulx showed photographs of the assaulted women, McCrimmon said he was going to be sick, and he was escorted to the washroom where he threw up. At this point, two hours after the interview had started, McCrimmon began to admit to his involvement in the investigated offences, following Sergeant Proulx's display of photographs taken by a store security camera. He subsequently made a number of statements implicating himself in the offences. The interview concluded at approximately 8:24 p.m. and McCrimmon was returned to his cell.

THE ISSUES

- Was McCrimmon afforded the right to retain and instruct counsel?
- Was the confession given by McCrimmon voluntary?

POINTS TO CONSIDER

- Section 10(b) of the Charter provides that "everyone has the right on arrest or detention to retain and instruct counsel without delay and to be informed of that right."
- McCrimmon was afforded the right to contact the lawyer of his choice. As noted, the lawyer was not in, and a message left on the lawyer's answering machine went unanswered.
- McCrimmon was given the choice of speaking with a Legal Aid "duty counsel." The conversation,

by phone, lasted about five minutes. The advice to McCrimmon was essentially to remain quiet in his interview with police.

- The interview room where McCrimmon was questioned was a confined space. He asked to be returned to his cell, but this request was denied.
- For a confession to be admitted in evidence in a criminal proceeding, it must be "voluntary." It cannot be forced. The rule relating to confessions is based on the common law. But, it also is reflected in the Charter provisions relating to a fair hearing, such as that contained in section 7 which provides: "Everyone has the right to life, liberty and security of the person and the right not to be deprived thereof except in accordance with principles of fundamental justice."

DISCUSSION

The case is *The Queen v. McCrimmon*, 2010, *Supreme Court Cases* 36. It was a companion case to *The Queen v. Sinclair.*

The incriminatory statements of McCrimmon (really statements of confession) were allowed by a majority of the Supreme Court of Canada. Chief Justice McLachlin and Justice Charron spoke for the Court majority. Justice Binnie concurred, and Justices LeBel, Fish, and Abella dissented.

MAJORITY DECISION

McCrimmon, said the Court majority, had the opportunity to seek counsel of his choice both in terms of his first choice and, later, in accepting the opportunity to speak with duty counsel for Legal Aid. Moreover, McCrimmon told the police that he was satisfied with the advice he was given.

What makes McCrimmon's case somewhat different is the question as to whether there were *changed circumstances in the course of the police interview.* More particularly, as the interview became more focused on the incidents reflecting the alleged crimes and McCrimmon's claim that he felt vulnerable and in need of counsel, were the police required to give him the right to speak with counsel at that point?

The majority opinion recognized this as a valid issue. But, the question remained whether, on the facts, McCrimmon's request was valid. This is what the majority opinion stated:

> In *Sinclair*, we explained that a single-occasion rule for consulting counsel will not always fulfill the purpose of section 10(b). A principled and purposive interpretation of the section 10(b) right to counsel requires that detainees should be able to speak to a lawyer again during the course of a custodial interrogation where [as was stated in Sinclair] *"a change in circumstances makes this necessary to fulfill the purpose of s. 10(b) of the Charter of providing the detainee with legal advice on his choice of whether to cooperate with the police investigation or decline to do so."* While we noted in *Sinclair* that the categories of situations in which a change in circumstances triggers a detainee's right to consult with counsel again are not closed, *we did identify three situations*

currently recognized in which section 10(b) requires a renewed right to consultation with counsel: new procedures involving the detainee; a change in the jeopardy facing the detainee; or reason to believe the first information provided was deficient. The question then becomes whether, in this case, there was a change of circumstances of this nature that made it necessary to provide Mr. McCrimmon with a further opportunity to consult with counsel to fulfill the purpose of section 10(b) [emphasis added].

We would also find no breach when Sergeant Proulx continued speaking to Mr. McCrimmon despite the latter's assertion, immediately when the discussion turned to the incidents in question, that he did not want to discuss the incidents under investigation until he had spoken with his lawyer.... At that point, Sergeant Proulx confirmed with Mr. McCrimmon that he understood it was his choice whether to say anything but that he, Sergeant Proulx, had a lot of information to provide and wanted to get to know Mr. McCrimmon....

Some ten minutes further into the discussion, Mr. McCrimmon stated that he wanted to speak to a lawyer, indicated that he would answer no further questions until he spoke to his own lawyer, and asked to go back to his cell.... Sergeant Proulx explained that it was his job to get to understand Mr. McCrimmon and to provide him with the facts. What followed was essentially a long monologue in which Sergeant Proulx continued to discuss the police investigation in relation to the incidents and tried to establish a rapport with Mr. McCrimmon in an attempt to persuade him to give his side of the story. During this portion of the interview, there was no objectively discernible change in circumstances which gave rise to Mr. McCrimmon's right to consult again with counsel.

Sergeant Proulx then proceeded to progressively reveal the evidence against Mr. McCrimmon. As described earlier, when pressed for his version of the events, Mr. McCrimmon emphasized the absence of his lawyer, expressing his sense of vulnerability without legal representation and his ignorance of the "'legal ways,'" and insisted that he would not speak without his lawyer.... As we discussed in *Sinclair*, the gradual revelation to the detainee of the evidence that incriminates him does not, without more, give rise under section 10(b) to a renewed right to consult with counsel. However, where developments in the investigation suggest that the detainee may be confused about his choices and right to remain silent, this may trigger the right to a renewed consultation with a lawyer under section 10(b).

Arguably, Mr. McCrimmon's expression of vulnerability and ignorance of the law, when considered in isolation, could indicate such confusion. However, when the circumstances are viewed as whole, it is clear that Mr. McCrimmon understood his right to silence. Sergeant Proulx repeatedly confirmed that it was Mr. McCrimmon's choice whether to speak or not. It is apparent from Mr. McCrimmon's interjections in the course of the interview that he understood this. As the trial judge put it: "He clearly discerned which questions might put him in jeopardy and indicated he did not wish to answer those questions."

We conclude that there were no changed circumstances during the course of the interrogation that required renewed consultation with a lawyer.

CONCURRING OPINION

Justice Binnie dissented in *Sinclair*, but he concurred with the majority opinion in *McCrimmon*. He agreed with the majority view that there were no changed circumstances arising in the police interview that objectively required the opportunity for McCrimmon to speak with counsel. Justice Binnie wrote:

There is nothing in the [interview] transcript to suggest that his requests were "reasonably justified by the objective circumstances." Mr. McCrimmon says that he wants "the opportunity to have [his] counsel present" and the officer responds that "there's law that says that doesn't happen." General questions about relations with sex workers follow. Mr. McCrimmon says "no comment" on several occasions, clearly understanding his right to silence. He again asks for his lawyer to be present, repeated at [transcript] p. 50, but at p. 52 the police officer says "you don't have to keep repeating it" and the interview proceeds for a further couple of hours or so without any further request to consult counsel. The officer's request not to "keep repeating it" may have been a factor in inhibiting further requests, but nowhere in the balance of the interrogation can Mr. McCrimmon flag a point in time or an issue on which a further consultation could be considered 'reasonably justified by the objective circumstances, which were or ought to have been apparent to the officer: [citing] *Sinclair*, at para. 80.

It follows that we reject Mr. McCrimmon's further argument that the trial judge's failure to recognize a breach of the right to counsel undermined his conclusion that the statement was voluntary. It is important to add, however, as we noted in *Sinclair*, that the continuation of an interview in the face of the detainee's repeated expression of his desire for the interview to end and to speak with counsel may raise a reasonable doubt as to the voluntariness of any subsequently given statement. However, it is clear from the trial judge's reasons that he considered all relevant circumstances in determining that the statements were voluntary, including any subjective impact the refusal of Mr. McCrimmon's requests to speak to counsel may have had on him. Consequently, we see no reason to interfere with the trial judge's conclusion on voluntariness.

DISSENT

Justices LeBel, Fish, and Abella carried forward their dissent in the Sinclair case: The right to counsel is constitutional. It is embedded in the Charter. It follows that any limitation on that right must be justified. That is, the burden is on the government to justify the limitation of the right to counsel. In that regard, the Court should be more attuned to the nature of custodial investigations — the so called "investigative interview." It is, said the dissent, a relentless interrogation of a confined suspect.

This is what the dissent, written by Justices LeBel and Fish and concurred with by Justice Abella, stated:

> Our particular concern here, as in the companion [appeal] of *Sinclair* ... is with the effective exercise of the right to counsel by detainees who are subjected to relentless

custodial interrogation, even after they have unequivocally and repeatedly invoked their right to silence or to counsel. Both rights, and their meaningful exercise, are integral aspects of a detainee's pre-trial protections under the Charter. The right to counsel is both fundamental and necessarily broad in scope. While the initial advice to simply keep quiet may suffice at the outset of an interrogation, more substantive advice and assistance may be required as the interrogation progresses.

We do not agree with our colleagues that detainees who, in this context, invoke their right to counsel in order to render more effective their right to silence can be denied either right on the ground that doing so would improperly frustrate the investigative interview. We do not believe that the right to consult counsel depends on the narrow and restrictive finding, in the opinion of the police interrogator, of a manifest or material change in jeopardy....

It is a limitation on the right to counsel, not the exercise of that right, that must be constitutionally justified. We reiterate our objection to any limitation on the s. 10(b) right without constitutional justification and evidence of necessity, and that would depend on the interrogator's exercise of discretion.

Moreover, a custodial interrogation by any other name remains just that.

Characterizing the relentless interrogation of a confined suspect as an "investigative interview" does not transform its true nature and sole purpose. An interview is a conversation between two or more consenting participants who are free to leave as they choose. A relentless custodial interrogation, on the other hand, is an attempt by police officers, who have total physical control of a detainee, to obtain an incriminating statement by systematically disregarding the detainee's express wish and declared intention not to speak with them. That is the exercise that concerns us here, as it did in *Sinclair*.

The decisive issue is whether the police can refuse to allow a detainee to consult counsel and, by pursuing their custodial interrogation, render ineffective the detainee's assertion of the right to silence. Our firm answer to that question is 'no, they cannot.'

Since detainees have no legal obligation to participate in a custodial interrogation, they can hardly be said to frustrate, impermissibly, any persistent attempts by the police to prevent them from exercising their constitutional right to counsel. There is no police right, under the common law or the Constitution, to the unfettered access to a detainee, for interrogation to the point of confession.

This case illustrates yet again why the right to counsel is not spent upon its initial exercise. It demonstrates the broader role played by counsel even within the relatively narrow confines of a custodial interrogation.

CHALLENGE QUESTION

AN OPPORTUNITY TO CHOOSE?

Stanley James Willier was arrested by police for murder. He was promptly and fully informed of his right to counsel and police facilitated a brief telephone conversation with duty counsel available through Legal Aid.

The next day, when offered another opportunity to speak with counsel, Willier made an unsuccessful attempt to reach a specific lawyer. He was told that the lawyer would not likely call him back before the next day. Police reminded him of the availability of duty counsel and Willier decided to speak with duty counsel a second time, although his preference was the lawyer he had earlier selected. The conversation lasted only a few minutes, after which Willier expressed satisfaction with the advice received. After a brief interval, the investigative interview began.

Q. For our purposes, can it be said that Willier had been given his section 10(b) rights under the Charter?

This reflects another companion case to *The Queen v. Sinclair* decided by the Supreme Court of Canada: *The Queen v. Willier*, 2010 *Supreme Court of Canada Cases* 37. There, a unanimous Supreme Court ruled that Willier had been given his section 10(b) rights. In one sense, the standard used in reaching the Court's decision, again one handed down by the chief justice and Justice Charron, was that *Willier had the choice to speak with police investigators that was both free and informed.* But, this should be added: Willier had an individual duty to act diligently in exercising his right to choose counsel — after having been informed of his right to do so.

For discussion purposes, we set out parts of the Court's decision:

> The informational duty imposed on the police is relatively straightforward. However, should a detainee positively indicate that he or she does not understand his or her right to counsel, the police cannot rely on a mechanical recitation of that right and must facilitate that understanding.
>
> In circumstances where a detainee has asserted his or her right to counsel and has been reasonably diligent in exercising it, yet has been unable to reach a lawyer because duty counsel is unavailable at the time of detention, courts must ensure that the Charter-protected right to counsel is not too easily waived. Indeed, I find that an additional informational obligation on police will be triggered once a detainee, who has previously asserted the right to counsel, indicates that he or she has changed his or her mind and no longer

wants legal advice. At this point, police will be required to tell the detainee of his or her right to a reasonable opportunity to contact a lawyer and of the obligation on the part of the police during this time not to take any statements or require the detainee to participate in any potentially incriminating process until he or she has had that reasonable opportunity. This additional informational requirement on police ensures that a detainee who persists in wanting to waive the right to counsel will know what it is that he or she is actually giving up.

Thus, when a detainee, diligent but unsuccessful in contacting counsel, changes his or her mind and decides not to pursue contact with a lawyer, section 10(b) mandates that the police explicitly inform the detainee of his or her right to a reasonable opportunity to contact counsel and of the police obligation to hold off in their questioning until then....

Detainees who choose to exercise their section 10(b) right by contacting a lawyer trigger the implementational duties of the police. These duties require the police to facilitate a reasonable opportunity for the detainee to contact counsel, and to refrain from questioning the detainee until that reasonable opportunity is provided. However, these obligations are contingent upon a detainee's reasonable diligence in attempting to contact counsel.... What constitutes reasonable diligence in the exercise of the right to contact counsel will depend on the context of the particular circumstances as a whole....

Such a limit on the rights of a detainee are necessary ... because without it, it would be possible to delay needlessly and with impunity an investigation and even, in certain cases, to allow for an essential piece of evidence to be lost, destroyed or rendered impossible to obtain. The rights set out in the Charter, and in particular the right to retain and instruct counsel, are not absolute and unlimited rights. They must be exercised in a way that is reconcilable with the needs of society.

Should detainees opt to exercise the right to counsel by speaking with a specific lawyer, section 10(b) entitles them to a reasonable opportunity to contact their chosen counsel prior to police questioning. If the chosen lawyer is not immediately available, detainees have the right to refuse to speak with other counsel and wait a reasonable amount of time for their lawyer of choice to respond. What amounts to a reasonable period of time depends on the circumstances as a whole, and may include factors such as the seriousness of the charge and the urgency of the investigation.... If the chosen lawyer cannot be available within a reasonable period of time, detainees are expected to exercise their right to counsel by calling another lawyer or the police duty to hold off will be suspended: *The Queen v. Ross*, [1989] 1 *Supreme Court of Canada Reports* 3. As Lamer J. emphasized in *Ross*, diligence must also accompany a detainee's exercise of the right to counsel of choice (pp. 10–11):

"Although an accused or detained person has the right to choose counsel, it must be noted that ... a detainee must be reasonably diligent in the exercise of these rights and if he is not, the correlative duties imposed on the police ... are suspended. Reasonable diligence in the exercise of the right to choose one's counsel depends upon the context facing the accused or detained person. On being arrested, for example, the detained person is faced with an immediate need for legal advice and must exercise reasonable diligence accordingly. By contrast, when seeking the best lawyer to conduct a trial, the accused person faces no such immediacy. Nevertheless, accused or detained persons have a right to choose their counsel and it is only if the lawyer chosen cannot be available within a reasonable time that the detainee or the accused should be expected to exercise the right to counsel by calling another lawyer."

WHAT IF?

Suppose a police confession is obtained in violation of section 10(b) of the Charter. Does it follow that the confession cannot be used in evidence in a later criminal trial?

It does not. The Charter conditions the exclusion of evidence obtained in violation of its provisions in section 24(2) which provides: "Where ... a court concludes that evidence was obtained in a manner that infringed or denied any rights or freedoms guaranteed by this Charter, the evidence shall be excluded if it is established that, having regard to all the circumstances, the admission of it in the proceedings would bring the administration of justice into disrepute."

In the McCrimmon case, discussed in "You Be the Judge: The Case of the Repeated Request," the dissent discussed the potential role of section 24(2). They stated:

> In determining whether the admission of evidence obtained by way of a Charter breach would bring the administration of justice into disrepute, the court must weigh three factors:
> (1) the seriousness of the Charter-infringing conduct;
> (2) the impact of the breach on the accused's Charter-protected rights and interests; and
> (3) society's interest in the adjudication of the case on its merits.
>
> Our analysis in *Sinclair* is equally applicable in this case. We nonetheless think it necessary to add the following observations.
>
> Sergeant Proulx (the police interrogator) proceeded on the basis of his understanding of the law as it stood at that time, and was therefore acting in good faith. However, like the interrogating officer in *Sinclair*, Sergeant Proulx acted

as if he was entitled to Mr. McCrimmon's statement — that he was entitled to have his side of the story. Sergeant Proulx therefore not only denied Mr. McCrimmon his right to counsel. In doing so, Sergeant Proulx also explicitly refused to accept and respect Mr. McCrimmon's assertion of his constitutionally-entrenched right to silence.

The officer's Charter-infringing conduct was therefore serious, and that conduct had a serious impact on Mr. McCrimmon's Charter rights.

Accordingly, we would exclude Mr. McCrimmon's statement pursuant to section 24(2) of the Charter.

CHALLENGE QUESTIONS

CONFESSIONS ON FALSE EVIDENCE

Suppose police use non-existent evidence to obtain a confession. For example, suppose police say to the person being questioned that they have an eyewitness who has definitely identified the person being interrogated as the shooter in a homicide. In fact, however, police do not have such a witness. They are using this "story" to obtain a confession — and they succeed. The person being interviewed confesses.

Q. Is there a risk that the confession may be ruled invalid on the ground that it may breach the rule allowing an individual to remain silent? Or, may the confession be ruled invalid in that it may deny the individual a further right to counsel?

There is a risk on both points. In the Sinclair case, the Court majority stated:

> We note that our colleagues LeBel and Fish JJ. express concern that these reasons in effect create "a new right on the part of the police to the unfettered and continuing access to the detainee for the purposes of conducting a custodial interview to the point of confession."
>
> We do not agree with the suggestion that our interpretation of section 10(b) will give [such power] to the police. This argument overlooks the requirement that confessions must be voluntary in the broad sense now recognized by the law. The police must not only fulfill their obligations under section 10(b); they must conduct the interview in strict conformity with the confessions rule. On this point, we disagree with Binnie J.... The confessions rule is broad-based and clearly encompasses the right to silence. Far from truncating [limiting] the detainee's constitutional right to silence, its recognition as one component of the common law rule enhances the right as any reasonable doubt on the question of voluntariness must result in the automatic exclusion of the statement....
>
> Our colleagues LeBel and Fish JJ. also assert that our approach is such that the detainee is effectively forced to participate in the police investigation. The suggestion is that the questioning of a suspect, in and

of itself, runs counter to the presumption of innocence and the protection against self-incrimination. This is clearly contrary to settled authority and practice.

In our view, in defining the contours of the section 7 right to silence and related Charter rights, consideration must be given not only to the protection of the rights of the accused but also to the societal interest in the investigation and solving of crimes. The police are charged with the duty to investigate alleged crimes and, in performing this duty, they necessarily have to make inquiries from relevant sources of information, including persons suspected of, or even charged with, committing the alleged crime. While the police must be respectful of an individual's Charter rights, a rule that would require the police to automatically retreat upon a detainee stating that he or she has nothing to say, in our respectful view, would not strike the proper balance between the public interest in the investigation of crimes and the suspect's interest in being left alone.

EDITORIAL COMMENT

The *Globe and Mail* made the following editorial comment on the *Sinclair* and *McCrimmon* cases under the title "A Right Diminished." The *Globe* critique was based on the paper's understanding of the right to counsel and to remain silent as set out in the Charter of Rights and Freedoms.

The right to counsel and the right to silence have been taken out to the parking lot and given a good working over — by the Supreme Court of Canada, no less. Both these rights are intimately connected to the core premise of Canadian justice: that the state bears the burden of proving an individual's guilt. Our highest court has unjustifiably and surprisingly weakened those rights.

In one case before the court, a British Columbia man accused of murder was put through several hours of interrogations, during which he repeatedly asked to speak with a lawyer. In a separate case, a B.C. man, accused of a series of assaults on women, tried over and over again to invoke his right to silence and a lawyer. In both cases, the men had spoken briefly, over the telephone, to a lawyer before being questioned. Having done so, they had, in effect, exhausted their right to counsel.

Section 10(b) of the Canadian Charter of Rights and Freedoms reads: "Everyone has the right on arrest or detention to retain and instruct counsel without delay and to be informed of that right." But a majority of the nine-member court — six judges — says that the initial phone call is enough, unless something has changed during the interrogation to justify another call. As for what that change is, consult a constitutional scholar — it is now beyond the average person's ability to understand. Simply being questioned for several hours in the middle of the night while being refused the right to return to one's cell is not deemed reason enough to have a lawyer present.

The only instruction that now makes sense for an anticipated interrogation, Mr. Justice Ian

Binnie wrote in dissent in one case, is "You have reached counsel. Keep your mouth shut. Press one to repeat the message."

Detainees have no legal obligation to participate in a custodial interrogation, other dissenters, going even further, said. How can they be in the wrong in asking for their constitutional right to counsel? The Charter's right to counsel, even the right to silence, no longer seems to say what it means. In practical terms, it will be easier for police to find incriminating information. But in the end, the Charter rights to silence and to counsel have been undermined (*Globe and Mail*, October 9, 2010).

YOU BE THE JUDGE

CITIZEN'S ARREST

Ordinarily, there is a public expectation that arrests are made by police. However, the law provides for what might seem to be an exception. Citizens seeing or experiencing a crime may make an arrest in the absence of police.

THE FACTS

It was May 23, 2009 in Toronto's Chinatown. On a video camera, David Chen, owner of the Lucky Moose Food Mart, spotted a shoplifter who had taken some plants (later valued at seventy-two dollars) and run away. About an hour later, the shoplifter returned. Chen approached him and asked for payment for the plants taken.

The alleged shoplifter, later identified as Anthony Bennett, refused. He ran from the store. Chen and two employees chased and caught him. They bound him and notified police. The Chinatown area had been the site of numerous shoplifting incidents. Frequently police were notified but, apparently because of the number of other calls received, they were not always able to respond promptly. In any event, Bennett was later charged by police and he pleaded guilty to shoplifting. He was sentenced to thirty days in jail.

Our concern, however, goes to charges pressed by police and the Crown against Chen. He found himself faced with charges of kidnapping, carrying a dangerous weapon (a box cutter), forcible confinement, and assault. His trial and court decision came a year later.

THE ISSUE

Did Chen make a lawful citizen's arrest?

POINTS TO CONSIDER

- If Chen were a security guard, he could do no more than make a citizen's arrest. So, the issue remains: Did Chen make a lawful citizen's arrest?
- Chen, with the help of his two employees, caught and restrained Bennett an hour after he allegedly took the plants from Chen's store. And, he caught Bennett in a chase from the store.

- Bennett resisted being restrained. He was tied and placed in a van by Chen and his two employees until police arrived in response to a call from Chen.
- A citizen's arrest generally must take place close in time to the commission of the claimed crime.

DISCUSSION

Justice Khawly, the trial judge, acquitted Chen. Before a crowded courtroom, he rejected the argument of the Crown that there was a time lapse between the first theft by Bennett and his later return to the store. If there were a substantial lapse, then it could be argued that Bennett really was in the process of committing a second crime — an offence apparently that he did not complete. If this theory were accepted, it followed that Chen had no power to make a citizen's arrest.

Justice Khawly called the Crown argument a "red herring." He deemed the return of Bennett to the store part of a "continuing theft — pure and simple." Thus, on the findings of fact, Chen was empowered to make a citizen's arrest.

More to the point, perhaps, the judgment of the court reflected the authority of the trial judge to make findings of fact which are difficult to overturn on appeal — unless they are clearly erroneous.

A LARGER PROBLEM?

Justice Khawly was sensitive to problems of theft in Chinatown and the difficulties of police in responding to shoplifting complaints. In a lengthy opinion, he asked: "Is Chen's community sending a message of vulnerability in the face of perceived police inaction? However unfair or unfounded, is that not really what stoked the embers of this case?"

Citing the "broken windows" theory, by which communities lose faith in the rule of law when minor crime goes unpunished, the judge suggested that Chen "tried to fill the void where the justice system failed," and asked if Chen could "after all, not be the canary in the coal mine?"

Mark Pugash, spokesman for Toronto police, said he understood the concern, but insisted that police take theft seriously; it's just a matter of prioritizing calls. He said:

> I have no doubt that if I were a merchant being plagued by that, I'd want to be able to pick up the phone and I'd want people to be there immediately, [but] most people understand we have to prioritize our calls. So if we get a call that you're getting beaten and we get another call that says, "Someone stole something from me," I think people would want us to treat crimes of violence or threat of violence more seriously."

A "LIMITED" GOVERNMENT RESPONSE?

The federal government responded to merchant concern for more police protection by an amendment to the Criminal Code in 2013. Referred to as the "Lucky Moose Bill," it allows citizens and store owners more leeway in protecting themselves and their property. For example, a citizen's arrest need not take place exactly at the time of the crime.

It could occur within a "reasonable time" of the crime, and if there is no police officer immediately available. Further, citizens and store owners can defend themselves if they believe they or their property are at "risk."

Obviously, there are questions that can arise:

- How much time is covered by "reasonable time"?
- What is the extent to which citizens or store owners may go in defending themselves or their property?

PROTECTING THE "VULNERABLE"

Police often are the individual's first point of contact with the criminal process. They investigate possible criminal violations, and they can detain, arrest, and lay charges against those believed to have violated the criminal law. Police can be seen as the community's first formal agency in bringing the accused to the "dock" — or not.

There are special rules binding on police in dealing with the young. For the most part, the rules for police conduct, or interface, with the young, are set out in the Youth Criminal Justice Act (YCJA).

As a preliminary matter, two points are made:

1. The rules of conduct for police under the YCJA are mandatory and police must follow them. If they fail to do so, they (or, more particularly, the Crown prosecutor) may find the case against the accused significantly weakened because evidence derived through improper police procedures might be thrown out by the court.
2. The YCJA, in its interpretation and enforcement, must conform to the Charter of Rights and Freedoms which, as we have noted, is part of the Constitution of Canada.

There is a protective shield for youths at the point when they are detained or arrested by police. That shield gives them greater rights than adults may claim under similar circumstances. The reasons underlying their establishment were set out by the Supreme Court of Canada in *L.T.H. v. The Queen*, 2008 *Supreme Court of Canada Reports* 49. Justice Fish, speaking for the seven-member Court majority, said:

> Young persons, even more than adults, are inclined to feel vulnerable when questioned by police officers who suspect them of crime and can influence their fate. Parliament has for that reason provided them by statute with a complementary set of enhanced procedural safeguards in §146 of the Youth Criminal Justice Act, Statutes of Canada 2002, chapter 1 (YCJA), which governs the admissibility of statements made to persons in authority by young persons who are accused of committing offences.

These rights apply to all young persons between the ages of twelve and eighteen. They are cast in terms of procedural rights — such as the right to have counsel and/or an adult present before making a statement to the police. The failure to comply with these procedural rights can have real consequences: The Crown may be denied the right to introduce such statements in evidence against the accused.

While the intent of the YCJA seems clear — protect "vulnerable" youngsters from police interrogation until they obtain the assistance of counsel or an adult — there are a number of questions that arose in the L.T.H. case. They include:

- What must police do to obtain a waiver of a young person's right to the assistance of counsel or an adult?

- Will a young person give up the right to counsel or the advice of an adult simply by making a clear statement to that effect?
- Can police assume that a young person knows his/her rights to counsel or assistance of an adult if that individual has had frequent contact with the police?
- Does the seriousness of the offence have any bearing on whether a trial judge will forgive police errors in obtaining a lawful waiver by a young person of the right to counsel or the advice of an adult?

THE FACTS OF *L.T.H. V. THE QUEEN*

By the time the Supreme Court of Canada handed down its decision in *L.T.H. v. The Queen*, the accused was no longer a youth within the meaning of the YCJA. He was nineteen, and it was four years after the events that gave rise to the Court's decision. (This "coming of age" — being a young offender at the time of arrest, and moving to adult status at the time of final judgment — is not unusual in YCJA criminal cases.)

L.T.H., then fifteen, was arrested in the early morning hours of August 8, 2004, by the RCMP in Cole Harbour, Nova Scotia, following a car chase that ended only when his car caught fire and was brought to a stop. Initially, L.T.H. was charged with dangerous driving. Then, he was transferred to the Halifax Regional Police Service where the charges against him increased. They included theft, possession of property obtained by crime, and failing to stop — as well as the original charge: dangerous driving.

L.T.H. was taken into custody by police at about 5:00 a.m. He was asked several times if he wanted the help of a lawyer. Each time, he refused such assistance.

Several hours after the arrest, L.T.H. was taken from the Cole Harbour police station to the Dartmouth police station where he slept for a few hours. Then he was transferred to the Halifax police station where he was interviewed by Constable Jeffrey Carlisle. The constable had a young offender police statement form that he reviewed with L.T.H.

It is important to note that the interview was videotaped; and that tape was made available by the Crown to the trial court judge, the appellate court, and, with the consent of Crown counsel and L.T.H.'s lawyer, to the Supreme Court of Canada, which reviewed it in the appeal that gave rise to the decision of the Court.

THE INTERVIEW AND THE WAIVER

This was not the first time that police had interviewed L.T.H. Indeed, in the hearing before the trial judge, L.T.H.'s mother said she had warned the police at the time of his arrest that her son had a learning disability — one which made it difficult for him to understand the questions put to him. She said that in earlier encounters with the police, it had been necessary for her to "explain" the questions and their meaning to her son.

Still, Constable Carlisle pressed on with the interview of L.T.H. He read from questions in the form that included a statement of an accused young offender's rights. He asked L.T.H. if he understood his rights. He answered: "Yes." The constable asked L.T.H. if he wanted to call a lawyer or talk with a lawyer in private. He answered: "No." L.T.H. also answered that he did not want a parent or "another appropriate adult" present while he was giving a statement or while he was questioned.

This is not to say that L.T.H. was "frozen" in his replies. He did assert himself. At one point, he interrupted Constable Carlisle's reading of the form and said he was "not going to answer all of the questions" asked.

Constable Carlisle responded that the questions were only of the "do-you-understand" type. L.T.H. raised no further objection to the questioning, and Constable Carlisle continued. He finished reading the "waiver-of-rights form," which L.T.H. initialed. L.T.H. then signed a waiver of rights.

At that point, police took a statement from L.T.H. who confessed to actions that formed the basis of the Crown's case against him.

A "TECHNICALITY"?

Counsel for L.T.H. challenged the waiver and the trial judge agreed. She ruled that the statement could not be received in evidence. The Crown presented no further evidence. The result: The charges against L.T.H. were dismissed. An acquittal was ordered.

The trial judge accepted that L.T.H.'s statement was voluntary. But, that was not enough. She said that the YCJA sets additional requirements for a youth to give a lawful waiver. In this regard, the trial judge said she was not convinced beyond a reasonable doubt that L.T.H. understood his rights and the consequences of waiving them.

The Crown appealed the decision of the trial judge. The Nova Scotia Court of Appeal allowed the appeal. It set aside the acquittal and ordered a new trial. The Court of Appeal ruled that the Crown must prove *beyond a reasonable doubt* that the young person was given a clear and proper statement of rights and choices under the YCJA.

But, said the Court of Appeal, the Crown does not have to prove that the young person in fact understood those rights. In this regard, the Court of Appeal acknowledged that actual (or subjective) understanding of such waiver rights is required by the YCJA.

But, having said this, it is another matter to state the level of proof required to show such understanding. That is, how does one prove actual understanding? Here, the Court of Appeal said that the Crown must prove waiver on a balance of probabilities. This is a lower standard of proof than beyond a reasonable doubt.

THE ROLE OF VIDEOTAPES

What role could the videotape play in the appeal of L.T.H.?

Section 146 of the YCJA requires that the statement of a young person be taken either by videotape or in writing. With L.T.H., the statement was taken by videotape.

The videotape would allow the Court to see the demeanour of the constable and L.T.H.. By that, we mean the Court could see some indications as to whether the constable intended to communicate with L.T.H. and if he succeeded in that regard.

The Court would see that the constable apparently intended not to make eye contact with L.T.H. Further, the Court would be able to see that the constable rushed the waiver questions. (If the waiver were based solely on the written statement, there would be no indication, as such, that the waiver questions were rushed.)

In terms of L.T.H., the videotape apparently allowed one to observe that L.T.H. did not seem to take the police interview seriously. This, in turn, allowed the Court to infer that, as a young offender, he was all the more in need of the advice of a lawyer and/or an adult. With more pointed and sensitive police questioning — especially after having been given some warning by L.T.H.'s mother concerning her son's learning difficulties — there might have been greater awareness of how much more was required to ascertain whether there had been any knowing waiver by L.T.H.

THE SUPREME COURT DECIDES

The decision in the L.T.H. case was appealed to the Supreme Court of Canada. The matter was heard and decided by a seven-member panel of the Court. All members of the panel agreed with the result, though three of the justices disagreed with the test that led to that result.

For all the justices, the issue to be decided was not one of "mere technicality." The statement of principles in the YCJA was quoted by Justice Fish, who spoke for the Court majority. He wrote:

> Section 3(b) of the YCJA ... provides that the criminal justice system for young persons must be separate from that of adults and emphasize the following ... (iii) enhanced procedural protection to ensure that young persons are treated fairly and that their rights, including their right to privacy, are protected.
>
> The procedural rights set out in §146 represent one instance of the enhanced protection Parliament has seen fit to provide for young persons. The relevant parts of §146 provide that no statement by a young person to a person in authority will be admissible in evidence against that young person unless: (1) the statement was voluntary (§146(2)(a)); (2) the person who took the statement "clearly explained to the young person, in language appropriate to his or her age and understanding," the young person's right to silence and right to consult counsel and another appropriate adult (and the requirement that any person consulted be present during the interview) (§146(2)(b)); and (3) the young person was given a reasonable opportunity to exercise those rights (§146(2)(c)).
>
> Finally, §146(4) provides that young persons, subject to certain conditions, can waive their right to consult counsel and an adult before making the statement and can also waive the right to have counsel and the adult present when the statement is made.

There is purpose to the procedural protections of the YCJA. Justice Fish recited the Court's view of Parliament's reasons for enacting section 146 of the YCJA. He wrote:

> This Court has consistently held that the rationale for §146, and its predecessor, lies in Parliament's recognition that young persons generally do not understand their legal rights as well as adults, are less likely to assert those rights in the face of a confrontation with a person in authority and are more susceptible to the pressures of interrogation.... *Given the purpose of the provision, it would be inconsistent to find that the statutory requirements of §146 will be complied with whenever a clearly worded form is read to a young person* [emphasis added].

> Even before the enactment of the YCJA and its predecessor, trial courts recognized that statements made by young persons should be treated differently than statements made by adults. In *The Queen v. Yensen*, [1961] *Ontario Reports* 703 (High Court), for example, McRuer (Chief Judge High Court) held that the interrogating officer must "demonstrate to the Court that the child did understand the caution as a result of careful explanation and pointing out to the child the consequences that may flow from making the statement."

RECOGNIZING REALITY

At the same time, Justice Fish said that the trial court should not turn its head away from reality. He wrote:

The requirement of understanding and appreciation applies to all young persons, including those who are no strangers to the criminal justice system. Section 146(2)(b) incorporates principles of fairness that must be applied uniformly to all without regard to the characteristics of the particular young person.

This does not mean that experience in the criminal justice system is irrelevant to the inquiry as to the young person's understanding. An individualized, objective approach must take into account the level of sophistication of the young detainee and other personal characteristics relevant to the young person's understanding.

Police officers, in determining the appropriate language to use in explaining a young person's rights, must therefore make a reasonable effort to become aware of significant factors of this sort, such as learning disabilities and previous experience with the criminal justice system.

In effect, the police are required to take the individual measure of the young person. Generalities, alone, will not do.

THE BASIS FOR THE MAJORITY TEST

It was the view of the majority in the L.T.H. case that the test of *beyond a reasonable doubt* set out in section 146 reflected both the common law and the requirements of section 10 of the Charter. This is how Justice Fish stated the matter:

Section 146 gives statutory expression to common law rules and constitutional rights that apply to adults and to young persons alike. It provides, for example, that no statement by a young person to a person in authority will be admissible in evidence against that young person unless it is voluntary. And it reaffirms the right to counsel enshrined in section 10 of the Canadian Charter of Rights and Freedoms.

Parliament has recognized in this way that the right to counsel and the right to silence are intimately related. And that relationship is underscored in §146 by the additional requirements that must be satisfied in order for statements made by young persons to be admissible against them at their trials. Parliament has in this way underscored the generally accepted proposition that procedural and evidentiary safeguards available to adults do not adequately protect young persons, who are presumed on account of their age and relative unsophistication to be more vulnerable than adults to suggestion, pressure and influence in the hands of police interrogators.

Accordingly, §146 provides that statements made by young persons are inadmissible against them unless the persons who took them "clearly explained to the young person, *in language appropriate to his or her age and understanding,*" the specific rights conferred by §146. This condition of admissibility has been referred to as the 'informational requirement' of §146 and it raises two questions that, again, are intimately related [emphasis added].

The first is whether the Crown must prove not only that the necessary explanation was given in appropriate and understandable language, but also that it was in fact understood by the young person who made the statement. The second is whether compliance with the informational requirement must be proved by the Crown beyond a reasonable doubt, or only on a balance of probabilities. Because of their interdependence, ... I would answer both questions together. In my view, the Crown's evidentiary burden will be discharged by clear and convincing evidence that the person to whom the statement was made took reasonable steps to ensure that the young person who made it understood his or her rights under §146 of the YCJA. A mere probability of compliance is incompatible with the object and scheme of §146, read as a whole. Compliance must be established beyond a reasonable doubt.

Finally, §146 provides that young persons, subject to certain conditions, can waive their right under that section to consult with counsel and an adult relative before making a statement and their right to have counsel and the relative present when the statement is made. As we shall see, an unbroken line of authority, beginning with *Korponay v. Attorney General of Canada*, [1982] 1 *Supreme Court of Canada Reports* 41, establishes that a waiver must be established by "clear and unequivocal [evidence] that the person is waiving the procedural safeguard and is doing so with full knowledge of the rights the procedure was enacted to protect and of the effect the waiver will have on those rights in the process".... Manifestly, where Parliament has specifically sought to endow young persons with enhanced procedural protections, this high standard has not been satisfied if the court is left with a reasonable doubt whether the requirements set out in *Korponay* and subsequently reaffirmed, have been met.

I hasten to add, however, that this exacting standard should not be taken to impose on the Crown a burden that it cannot properly be expected to discharge. Where compliance with the informational component is established beyond a reasonable doubt, the trial judge will be entitled — and, indeed, expected — to infer, in the absence of evidence to the contrary, that the young person in fact understood his or her rights under §146.

In this case, the trial judge was not satisfied that the Crown discharged its burden under §146 of the YCJA. She therefore found the appellant's statement inadmissible and ultimately entered an acquittal. The Court of Appeal disagreed. For the foregoing reasons, and the reasons that follow, I would allow the appeal and restore the appellant's acquittal at trial.

IN CONCLUSION

Courts can and do review police investigations, especially where questions arise as to whether police have complied with rights afforded all Canadians under the Charter of Rights and Freedoms. In general, it might be said that court review means looking to the reality of what happened — not to the legalisms, but to the real facts. For example, it doesn't matter that police might call their questioning of what amounts to be a suspect merely an informational chat when the reality is that the "chat" is in-depth questioning.

The burden to provide real Charter rights is not placed solely on the police. The person being questioned must assert his or her own claim, for example, to the right to counsel — once police have made it known (as they must) that such a right exists.

Finally, it must be understood that the Charter does not void, as such, any police violation of rights afforded all Canadians. Recall section 24(b) of the Charter that provides: "Where ... a court concludes that evidence was obtained in a manner that infringed or denied any rights or freedoms guaranteed by this Charter, the evidence shall be excluded if it is established that, having regard to all the circumstances, the admission of it in the proceedings would bring the administration of justice into disrepute."

REFERENCES AND FURTHER READING

* Cited by the Supreme Court of Canada

Allen, Ronald J. "Miranda's Hollow Core." *Northwestern University Law Review* 100 (2006): 71.*

Appleby, Timothy. "Toronto Shopkeeper Welcomes Changes to Citizen's Arrest Laws." *Globe and Mail*, February 17, 2011.

"A Right Diminished." *Globe and Mail*, October 9, 2010.

Bailey, Ian. "Cops with Cameras Future of Policing — Vancouver Chief." *Globe and Mail*, December 20, 2009.

Cassell, Paul G. "Miranda's Social Cost: An Empirical Reassessment." *Northwestern University Law Review* 90 (1995–95): 387.*

Cassell, Paul G. and Bret S. Hayman. "Police Interrogation in the 1990s: An Empirical Study of the Effects of Miranda." *U.C.L.A. Law Review* 43(1995–96): 839.*

Cassell, Paul G. and Richard Fowles. "Handcuffing the Cops? A Thirty-Year Perspective on Miranda's Harmful Effects on Law Enforcement." *Stanford Law Review* 50 (1997–98): 1055.*

"Citizen's Arrest Canada: New Rules Come Into Effect." Canadian Press, March 11, 2013.

Godsey, Mark A. "Reformulating the Miranda Warnings in Light of Contemporary Law and Understandings." *Minnesota Law Review* 90 (2006): 781.*

Leo, Richard A. "Inside the Interrogation Room." *Journal of Law and Criminology* 86 (1996): 266.*

Makin, Kirk. "No Right to Counsel During Interrogation." *Globe and Mail,* October 9, 2010.

Newfoundland and Labrador. *The Lamer Commission of Inquiry in the Proceedings Pertaining to: Ronald Dalton, Gregory Parsons and Randy Druken: Report and Annexes,* St. Johns: Government of Newfoundland and Labrador (2006).*

"No Right to Counsel in Police Interview: Top Court." *CBC.ca,* October 8, 2010.

Reinhart, Anthony and Anna Mehler Papering. "Shopkeeper Learns His Lesson in Acquittal." *Globe and Mail,* October 29, 2010.

Schulhofer, Stephen J. "Miranda's Practical Effect: Substantial Benefits and Vanishingly Small Social Costs." *Northwestern University Law Review* 90 (1996): 500.*

Stewart, Hamish. "The Confessions Rule and the Charter." *McGill Law Journal* 54 (2009): 417.*

Stuesser, Lee. "The Accused's Right to Silence: No Doesn't Mean No." *Manitoba Law Journal* 29 (2002): 149.*

Tibbetts, Janice. "No Right to Lawyer During Police Interrogation: Supreme Court." *National Post,* October 9, 2010.

"Toronto Chinatown Grocer Found Not Guilty." *CBC.ca,* October 29, 2010.

Ward, John. "No Right to a Lawyer During Interrogation, Supreme Court Rules." *Globe and Mail,* October 8, 2010.

Weisselberg, Charles D. "Mourning Miranda." *California Law Review* 96 (2008): 1519.*

Younger, Evelle J. "Results of a Survey Conducted in the District Attorney's Office of Los Angeles County Regarding Effect of the Miranda Decision upon the Prosecution of Felony Cases." *American Criminal Law Quarterly* 5 (1966–67): 32.*

CHAPTER 2

UNSEEN SEARCHES

How can there be a search without a search warrant? How can police obtain information about a suspect without that person's knowledge, with only the police being aware of the facts gathered?

Here we are not speaking of banking information or the kind of data one submits in completing required information such as tax returns. Think, for example, of the use of aircraft or drones equipped with special cameras and other equipment that can peer inside a home or an office. They can then test for and gather information relating to activity, or the inference of activity, such as the use of electricity far beyond that normally required for similar homes or offices. A question that arises is whether such information can be used to present to a judicial officer in order to obtain a search warrant for police to enter that home or office and search for drug manufacture.

The lead case in this chapter, *The Queen v. Walter Tessling*, [2004] 3 *Supreme Court of Canada Reports* 432, was used by police to support a request for a search warrant that was granted and, in turn, led to finding illicit drugs. Charges were laid and a conviction obtained. The facts of that case will be set out shortly. Again, it must be emphasized that the initial information obtained by the police was secured without a search warrant.

Government, including the police, is bound by the Charter of Rights and Freedoms, part of the Constitution of Canada. Section 8 of the Charter provides: "Everyone has the right to be secure against unreasonable search and seizure." However, the Charter also provides that even unlawfully obtained evidence can be used in criminal proceedings if it does not bring the administration of justice into disrepute (section 24).

We will find, however, that in the Tessling case, as well as in cases featured in the "You Be the Judge" exercise in this chapter, the primary question for the most part is whether the initial gathering of information, in itself, was a search and thus subject to the requirements of section 8 of the Charter. The government took the view that the information gathered was not private to the accused. Rather, it was public, and thus available to all — if they only had the devices to obtain it.

In *Tessling*, the trial court allowed the use of the contested information to obtain a search warrant that led to charges and conviction. The Ontario Court of Appeal ruled that the evidence initially obtained by the police was improper. It set aside the conviction. However, the Supreme Court reversed the ruling of the Court of Appeal and sustained the decision of the trial court.

Among the questions raised in this chapter are:

- Is there a single test for determining whether information is protected by the safeguards of section 8 of the Charter against unreasonable search and seizure?
- What role does the "privacy" of the individual play in defining search criteria?
- On what basis is "privacy" defined? Does the law of search and seizure look to whether, as a hypothetical matter, one's privacy might be invaded by a warrantless search? Or, is the question of whether a search has occurred based on the "here and now" facts, rather than how the science of probing might develop?

You will find that the Court places considerable emphasis on the facts of each case both in developing and applying principles of law: The "You Be the Judge" exercises feature cases which came before the Supreme Court of Canada. The first case, concerning a marijuana grow-op, deals with police access to utility company records disclosing how much electricity the accused used, and how that total compared with homes of comparable size in the community. The second case concerns police installation of a video "bug" in a hotel room to gather evidence of illegal gambling. Now, on to the facts of *Tessling*.

THE FACTS OF *THE QUEEN V. TESSLING*

In February of 1999, the RCMP began investigating the accused and, in particular, his home in Kingsville, a small town in southern Ontario. Two informants had reported to police that the accused and a "colleague" called Ken were producing and trafficking in marijuana (a controlled substance). One informant, the RCMP stated, was a "source whose credibility was untested." The second informant, however, was one the RCMP characterized as a "proven source." That person told the RCMP that a known drug dealer was buying large quantities of drugs from Ken in the area where the accused lived. But, the second informant did not directly tie the accused with the alleged drug transactions.

The RCMP contacted Ontario Hydro to find out if there was any unusual electricity usage at the properties owned by the accused or Ken. But the reply from Ontario Hydro was that, according to the metered supply, electricity usage was normal. The police then did visual surveillance of the questioned properties. The results were negative. Nothing suggested a marijuana grow-op. Still, the investigation continued.

The RCMP then used a thermal imaging device to take a "heat" picture of the home of the accused from an overhead aircraft. The camera, using Forward Looking Infra-Red (FLIR) technology, recorded not patterns of light but the distribution of heat over the surface of the building. The RCMP did not obtain a search warrant for the overflight.

The FLIR camera cannot "see" through the external surfaces of a building. (It is "off-the-wall" as opposed to "through-the-wall" technology.) However, the substantial amounts of heat generated by marijuana growing operations must eventually escape from the building. The FLIR camera creates an image of the distribution of escaping heat at a level of detail not apparent to the naked eye.

A FLIR image, put together with other information, can help the police get reasonable and probable grounds to believe that a marijuana growing operation is in residence. And that standard, once met, is enough to satisfy a court in granting a search warrant.

And so it was in this case. The RCMP were able to obtain a warrant based on the results of the FLIR image of the home of the accused, coupled with the information supplied by the two informants. When the RCMP entered the home, they found a large quantity of marijuana, two sets of scales, freezer bags, and several guns.

The street value of the marijuana was between $15,000 and $22,500. The accused was charged with a variety of offences, to which his response was that the FLIR overflight was a violation of his Charter rights and that the police should therefore never have been granted a search warrant based in part on the FLIR image. Accordingly, in the absence of a valid search warrant, he argued that the evidence obtained by the police from inside the house should be excluded. Since there was then insufficient evidence to support the convictions, he argued that he should be acquitted.

THE SUPREME COURT DECIDES

The central issue in the Tessling case is whether the FLIR overflight was a search within the meaning of section 8 of the Charter.

(In this regard, bear in mind that Charter rights are those granted to individuals against government action.) To answer that question, the Supreme Court first set out the value, or interest, that section 8 is designed to protect. Broadly stated, the Court held, in a unanimous opinion by Justice Binnie, that the interest held is privacy — restraints imposed on government with regard to prying into the lives of citizens. This is a value, the Court has declared, that "goes to the essence of a democratic state." Justice Binnie stated:

> Few things are as important to our way of life as the amount of power allowed the police to invade the homes, privacy and even the bodily integrity of members of Canadian society without judicial authorization. As La Forest J. stated in *The Queen v. Dyment*, [1988] 2 *Supreme Court of Canada Reports* 417, at pp. 427–28, "the restraints imposed on government to pry into the lives of the citizen go to the essence of a democratic state."
>
> The midnight knock on the door is the nightmare image of the police state. Thus it was in 1763 that, in a speech before the British Parliament, William Pitt (the Elder) famously extolled the right of everyone to exclude from his private domain the forces of the King: "The poorest man may in his cottage bid defiance to all the forces of the crown. It may be frail; its roof may shake; the wind may blow through it; the storm may enter, the rain may enter, but the King of England cannot enter! All his force dares not cross the threshold of the ruined tenement!"
>
> It is perhaps a long spiritual journey from Pitt's ringing pronouncements to [Tessling's] attempt to shelter a marijuana grow-op in the basement of

his home in Kingsville, Ontario, but the principle is the same. Building upon the foundation laid by the common law, section 8 of the Charter creates for "everyone" certain areas of personal autonomy where "all the forces of the Crown" cannot enter. These areas we have now gathered up under the general heading of privacy.

STRIKING A BALANCE: PRIVACY AND COMMUNITY PROTECTION

The history of the protection of individual privacy has its roots in the law of private property and trespass. Government agents might watch from a distance, but if the curtains of the home are drawn (or the drawbridge of the castle pulled), they had no right to enter without a warrant. The agents of government had no way of finding out what went on inside the home (or the castle). Yet, the Supreme Court noted:

> As technology developed, the protection offered by property rights diminished. Wiretaps, for example, require no physical intrusion, but can be implemented at a distance. FLIR images can be taken from an airplane. The courts were reluctant to accept the idea that, as technology developed, the sphere of protection for private life must shrink. Instead, it was recognized that the rights of private property were to some extent a proxy for the privacy that ownership of property originally conferred, and therefore, as the State's technical capacity for peeking and snooping increased, the idea of a protected sphere of privacy was refined and developed. The perspective adopted by the Court ... accordingly, is that

section 8 "protects people, not places."

But privacy is not the sum total for passing on the legality of government searches. There is another, sometimes countervailing, legitimate societal goal: safety, security, and the suppression of crime. The right to privacy may have to be weighed and balanced against the need for societal security. Justice Binnie cited an earlier decision of the Supreme Court of Canada in which it was stated: "An assessment must be made as to whether in a particular situation the public's interest in being left alone by government must give way to the government's interest in intruding on the individual's privacy in order to advance its goals, notably those of law enforcement."

But, how is that balance to be determined? Justice Binnie, citing other Supreme Court decisions, said the primary approach should be determining under all the circumstances — that is, the facts of the case — just what were the individual's reasonable expectations of privacy. And, such a determination must be made based on: (1) what the individual subjectively believed, and (2) the "objective reasonableness of the expectation."

PRIVACY INTERESTS

How these tests or principles will be applied in part is determined by looking at the particular privacy interest involved. That is, one privacy interest may have a higher claim for protection than another interest. In this regard, the Court listed three kinds of privacy interests: personal, territorial, and informational. Let's examine each interest to get an idea of the scope of protection. But, in doing this, it is also important to recognize that the facts of any one case may bring an overlap between interests. In *Tessling,* the facts centred on an overflight of Tessling's home to measure escaping heat. Tessling himself was not the subject of a search without a warrant.

1. Personal privacy. This, said Justice Binnie, has the strongest

claim to constitutional protection because it protects bodily integrity and, in particular, the right not to have our bodies touched or explored to disclose objects or matters we wish to conceal. Thus, Justice Binnie continued: "The State cannot conduct warrantless strip searches unless they are incident to a lawful arrest and performed in a reasonable manner ... in circumstances where the police have reasonable and probable grounds for concluding that a strip search is necessary in the particular circumstances of the arrest.... Nor may the police take bodily samples without authorization."

2. Territorial privacy. This also has a high claim to protection. Its centre is the home which legal tradition, cited above, has long protected against warrantless searches. Yet, move from the home to other "territory" and the intensity of protection may shrink. For example, the perimeter of the home may have less protection than the home itself. Still, the central inquiry remains: What is reasonable in terms an expectation of privacy? That expectation may be less if the object is a private car, or a school locker, or (at the end of the spectrum) a jail cell.

3. Informational privacy. Justice Binnie called this subject a "thorny question." Its subject relates to "how much information about ourselves and activities we are entitled to shield from the curious eyes of the state." The start point under the Charter seems to be the assumption that all information about a person is in a fundamental way that of the individual, to communicate or retain as that person sees fit.

In the final analysis, these three interest zones are not cast in concrete. Rather, they are tools to analyze cases. Justice Binnie wrote: "The distinction between personal, territorial and informational privacy provides useful analytical tools, but of course in a given case, the privacy interest may overlap the categories. Here [in *Tessling*], for example, the privacy interest is essentially informational (i.e. about [Tessling's] activities) but it also implicates his territorial privacy because although the police did not actually enter his house, that is where the activities of interest to them took place."

DRAWING A REASONABLENESS LINE

Justice Binnie related the expectation of privacy to the underlying values of the Charter: individual dignity, integrity, and autonomy. He said that information impacts on these values to the extent that it relates to a biographical core of personal information. And, partly because both the facts and the technology involving such information keeps changing, Justice Binnie said that the focus of the Court should be the whole of individual fact situations as they occurred.

As noted, present FLIR technology detects only external surface heat. Justice Binnie put some emphasis on current FLIR technology. But, it was such technology which the Court was asked to pass upon. And, in that regard, Justice Binnie stated:

> The information obtained via a FLIR image by itself cannot provide sufficient grounds to obtain a search warrant. This is because, as the Crown acknowledges, the relative crudity of the present technology does not, in itself, permit any inferences about the precise activity giving rise to the heat. For that, other evidence is required to determine if there is any reason to believe the source of the heat is a marijuana grow-op. As Crown counsel put the point in oral argument, the process of obtaining a search warrant sits "on a fulcrum. And you pile straws on one side. And this [FLIR image] is one of the straws." Moreover, "if you don't have a number of other cogent items of evidence, [FLIR] isn't going to help you greatly." Based on current FLIR technology, this is correct.

Tessling did not testify on his application to exclude the evidence resulting from the search. Still, Justice Binnie, for the Court, agreed with the decision of the Court of Appeal: "It may be presumed unless the contrary is shown in a particular case that information about what happens inside the home is regarded by the occupants as private. Such an expectation is rooted in the ancient law of trespass and finds its modern justification in the intimacies of personal and family life. This is the approach adopted by the Ontario Court of Appeal and, so far as it goes, I agree with it."

Yet, and this was important to the decision in *Tessling*, it was the heat pattern on the outside of the home which FLIR measured. That pattern did not tell the police what, as such, happened inside the home. Rather, it allowed an inference to be drawn that marijuana could be raised there with the use of intense lighting. Police needed more than evidence of external heat patterns to obtain a search warrant. Thus, the Court could find a subjective interest in Tessling's privacy as to what went on inside his home but, at the same time, allow evidence of the external heat pattern. But, even here, the absence of subjective expectation of privacy may not end the matter.

This is how Justice Binnie put the matter:

> However, I do not think it can be said that "allowing" heat to escape rebuts an expectation of privacy in the way, for example, that the accused was said to "abandon" his privacy interest in the garbage he put out on the street for collection in *The Queen v. Joyce*, [1996] 95 *Ontario Appellate Court Cases* 321 (C.A.), at paras. 4–5. Few people think to conceal their home's heat loss profile, and would have difficulty doing so if they tried. Living as he does in a land of melting snow and spotty home insulation, I do not believe that the respondent had a serious privacy interest in the heat patterns on the exposed external walls of his home. However, the police

were clearly interested in the "heat profile" not for its own sake but for what it might reveal about the activities inside the home. In that respect, to the extent that it is in issue, the respondent maintained a subjective expectation of privacy.

I should add a caveat [caution]. *The subjective expectation of privacy is important but its absence should not be used too quickly to undermine the protection afforded by section 8 to the values of a free and democratic society.* In an age of expanding means for snooping readily available on the retail market, ordinary people may come to fear (with or without justification) that their telephones are wiretapped or their private correspondence is being read [emphasis added].

DECISION

The Court allowed evidence of the FLIR results to be used in obtaining a warrant to search Tessling's home. And the evidence there obtained was properly admissible at his trial, with the result that his conviction was restored. Again, however, much of the emphasis in Justice Binnie's opinion was on the fact that the FLIR test measured the outside of the home and, as such, allowed only for inferences as to what might have occurred inside the home. In that regard, more was required to support the request for a warrant. And that additional information came largely from an informant. Our concern in this case has been with the legality of using the FLIR overflight results without a warrant.

Justice Binnie, for the Court, stated:

> The marijuana grow-op itself was certainly not in public view. Thus the debate is forced back to the same question posed at the outset: What exactly

does the FLIR image tell the police about the existence of a marijuana grow-op inside the house? The answer, as discussed, is that FLIR imaging cannot identify the source of the heat or the nature of the activity that created it. It merely tells the police that there are heat-generating activities within the home. (It would be strange if it were otherwise.) The existence and distribution of heat on the external walls is consistent with a number of hypotheses including as one possibility the existence of a marijuana grow-op. FLIR's usefulness depends on what other information the police have.

While I conceptualize the subject matter somewhat differently than Abella J.A. [who handed down the appellate court decision] as externally obtained information about the home (because no "intrusion" in any meaningful sense is possible under existing FLIR technology), I agree with the concern that privacy is closely linked to the effect that a breach of that privacy would have on the freedom and dignity of the individual ... [and that] we must always be alert to the fact that modern methods of electronic surveillance have the potential, if uncontrolled, to annihilate privacy....

For reasons already stated, I do not regard the use of current FLIR technology as the functional equivalent of placing the police inside the home. Nor is it helpful in the Canadian context to compare the state of technology in 2004 with that which existed at Confederation in 1867, or in 1982 when section 8 of the Charter was adopted.

Having regard to its purpose, I do not accept that section 8 is triggered by a FLIR image that discloses that heat sources of some unknown description are present inside the structure, or that the heat distribution is uneven. Certainly FLIR imaging generates information about the home but section 8 protects people, not places. The information generated by FLIR imaging about the respondent does not touch on a biographical core of personal information, nor does it tend to reveal intimate details of [Tessling's] lifestyle.... It shows that some of the activities in the house generate heat. That is not enough to get [Tessling] over the constitutional threshold.

External patterns of heat distribution on the external surfaces of a house is not information in which [Tessling] had a reasonable expectation of privacy. The heat distribution, as stated, offers no insight into his private life, and reveals nothing of his biographical core of personal information. Its disclosure scarcely affects the dignity, integrity and autonomy of the person whose house is subject of the FLIR image.

YOU BE THE JUDGE

PUBLIC OR PRIVATE INFORMATION?

The case that follows is real. The issues centre around validity of the investigation and search by police leading up to the charges laid and the evidence presented at trial.

THE FACTS

Robert Scott Plant of Calgary, Alberta, was charged with unlawful cultivation of marijuana contrary to section 6(1) of the Narcotic Control Act (NCA). He was convicted on that charge. However, he was acquitted on the charge of possession of marijuana for the purposes of trafficking under section 4(2) of the NCA. It is the investigation leading up to the search of Plant's home that is of concern to us.

The Calgary Police Service received an anonymous Crime Stoppers tip. The caller said that marijuana was being grown in what the caller described as a "cute house" next to another house "with a lot of windows" on 26th Street between two consecutive cross avenues in Calgary.

Police conducted a "reconnaissance" which included travelling along the reported street. They believed they identified the specific address. A member of the police drug unit used a police computer terminal linked to the main frame of Calgary's utility company. After entering a police department password, the computer link allowed police to obtain comparative electricity consumption data both as to the home in question and two similar area homes. That data indicated that, over a six-month period, the home in question used four times the amount of electricity compared to two similar homes.

Two members of the drug squad, in plain clothes, then went to the home. They knocked on the front door. There was no answer. They then walked to the back door. As they walked, they noticed two basement windows covered with something "opaque." They saw what appeared to be the outside vent for a dryer. They sniffed, and smelled nothing. But the vent, they saw, was plugged with a plastic bag. This, based on their experience, was "consistent" with other marijuana hydroponic operations. The two officers were chased from the premises by a nearby resident who had returned home. One of the two officers returned to his detachment and prepared a search warrant, summarizing the information obtained. The warrant was issued by a provincial court judge, and carried out by eight officers. Police found 112 marijuana seedling plants.

THE ISSUES

- Without a search warrant, was the "perimeter" walk around the residence of the accused lawful?
- Without a search warrant, was police access and use of electrical utility computer information lawful?
- Even if the search were unlawful, could the results still be used in evidence in a criminal proceeding under section 24(2) of the Charter?

POINTS TO CONSIDER

- Section 12 of the Narcotic Control Act (NCA) allows police to "enter and search any place *other than a dwelling-house* without a search warrant if they have reasonable grounds to believe that an offence under the NCA has been committed" [emphasis added].
- Section 8 of the Charter of Rights and Freedoms provides that "everyone has the right to be secure against unreasonable search or seizure."

- The purpose of section 8 of the Charter is to protect individual privacy from the state. The police obtained ongoing access to consumer electricity utility use as a result of an agreement between the police and the utility company.
- There must be reasonable cause to believe that a violation of the NCA has been committed for a search warrant to be issued. It is possible to strike one unlawful basis for issuing a search warrant and still sustain it — so long as the remaining lawful information is sufficient to permit a warrant.
- A tip can be used to support a request for a search warrant if it has a basis in "reliability" which can be assessed in part by the accuracy of the tip.

DISCUSSION

This exercise is based largely on *The Queen v. Plant*, [1993] 3 *Supreme Court Reports* 281, decided by a seven-member panel of the Supreme Court of Canada. The decision, which allowed the results flowing from the search warrant to be used in the criminal trial, was handed down by Justice John Sopinka. Justice McLachlin (later chief justice) agreed with much of Justice Sopinka's reasoning and the result reached by the Court. However, she would have ruled the computer records of the utility company as private and subject to the requirements of section 8 of the Charter.

We begin our discussion with this: If the search warrant were unlawful and that which flowed from it could not otherwise be saved by section 24(2) of the Charter, then

Plant would have to be acquitted. The evidence that convicted him came from the search of his home, namely the marijuana seedlings found in his basement.

THE COMPUTER RECORDS

The computer records, even if they were properly obtained by the police, did not, in themselves, demonstrate that marijuana had been grown. Such records only show that the amount of electricity necessary to power light for such growing had been used. In itself, it is not enough for a judge to issue a search warrant. Additional information is needed to show that an NCA violation has taken place, such as a specific claim that the accused has, in fact, grown marijuana.

For the police in the Plant case, that claim came from the tipster, about whom more will be said shortly. Again, to issue a search warrant, the judge must find that the information supporting it reasonably shows that a violation of the NCA has taken place (in this case, growing marijuana).

Now, however, let us return to the computer records, knowing that they are important but not determinative to the issuance of a search warrant. The central question in *Plant* was whether those records were private or public. If they were public, then the law relating to search warrants was not applicable — they were subject to seizure by the police. The reason: In law, no search within the meaning of section 8 of the Charter would have taken place.

Justice Sopinka held that the utility company records were public and, as such, were properly accessed by the police. Another way of expressing this conclusion is to say that the records were not confidential to Plant. It could not be said that Plant had any reasonable expectation as to the privacy of the records. And, against any expectation of privacy must be measured the interest of the state in law enforcement. Justice Sopinka stated:

> The purpose of section 8 [of the Charter] is to protect against intrusion of the state on an individual's privacy. The limits on such state action are determined by balancing the right of citizens to have respected a reasonable expectation of privacy as against the state interest in law enforcement....
>
> In balancing the reasonable expectation of privacy of the individual with the interests of the state in law enforcement, this Court has determined that electronic taping of private communication by state authorities violates the personal sphere protected by section 8 [of the Charter].... And seizure by state agents of a blood sample taken by medical personnel for medical purposes ... has been found to run afoul of the section 8 right against unreasonable search and seizure in that the dignity, integrity and autonomy of the individual are directly compromised. While this Court has considered the possibility of violations of section 8 in relation to informational privacy ... we have not previously considered whether state inspection of computer records implicates section 8 of the Charter....
>
> In fostering the underlying values of dignity, integrity, and autonomy, it is

fitting that section 8 of the Charter should seek to protect a biographical core of personal information which individuals in a free and democratic society would wish to maintain and control from dissemination to the state. This would include information which tends to reveal intimate details of the lifestyle and personal choices of the individual. The computer records investigated in [this] case ... while revealing the pattern of electricity consumption in the residence cannot reasonably be said to reveal intimate details of [Plant's] life since electricity consumption reveals very little about the personal lifestyle or private decisions of the occupant of the residence.

The nature of the relationship between [Plant] and the [utility] Commission cannot be characterized as a relationship of confidence. The Commission prepared the records as part of an ongoing commercial relationship and there is no evidence that it was contractually bound to keep them confidential. This is not to suggest that records prepared in a commercial context can never be subject to the privacy protection afforded by section 8 of the Charter. If commercial records contain material which meets [a] personal and confidential standard ... the commercial nature of the relationship between the parties will not necessarily foreclose a section 8 claim.

Although it has been indicated that some utilities commissions have developed policies against releasing consumption information to police ... it was clearly the policy of the Calgary Commission to permit police access to the computer data bank, albeit through a computer password. Further, it is generally possible for an individual to inquire with respect to the energy consumption at a particular address, so that this information is subject to inspection by members of the public at large. The accessibility of the information to the public is, in my view, more relevant to the issue than the policy of release developed by the Calgary Commission since the primary concern in this analysis is the expectation of privacy held by the person whose information was released, rather than the manner in which the body releasing the information categorized it. Nevertheless, I do not view the relevant relationship in [this] case ... as one which is reasonably characterized as confidential.

The place and manner in which the information in [this] case was retrieved also point toward the conclusion that [Plant] held no reasonable expectation of privacy with respect to the computerized electricity records. The police were able to obtain the information on-line by agreement of the Commission. Accessing the information did not involve intrusion into places ordinarily considered private.... Nor did it involve invasion by state agents in personal computer records confidentially maintained by a private citizen. While the requirement that the police use a password to access the information may suggest some element of privacy in the manner in which the search was conducted, it may equally suggest that the password was merely intended to ensure that on-line information was available only to the police. In any event, the search was not conducted in an intrusive or high-handed manner, so that on balance, I would conclude that the place and manner of the search were in keeping with what could reasonably have been expected by [Plant].

In addition to the fact that the manner and place of the search are indicative of a minimally intrusive search, the seriousness of the offence militates in favour of the conclusion that the requirements of law enforcement outweigh the privacy interest claimed by [Plant]. As this Court previously concluded ... while participation in the illicit trade of marijuana may not be as serious as the trade in other narcotics such as cocaine, it remains an offence which is taken seriously by law enforcement agents.

Overall, I have concluded from the nature of the information, the relationship between the appellant and the Commission, the place and manner of the search, and the seriousness of the offence under investigation, that [Plant] cannot be said to have held a reasonable expectation of privacy in relation to the computerized electricity records which outweighs the state interest in enforcing the laws relating to narcotics offences. As such, [Plant] has failed to bring this search within the parameters of section 8 of the Charter. This information was, therefore, available to the police to support the application for a search warrant.

THE TIPSTER: NEEDED INFORMATION

An anonymous tip to police can support a search warrant if it is seen as reliable. There are three tests, Justice Sopinka said, for reliability:

1. Was the information predicting the criminal offence compelling?
2. If the source (as in *Plant*) came from outside the police, was it compelling?
3. Was the tip supported by police investigation before the decision to conduct the search?

Justice Sopinka found that the tests had been met, and that the tip could form part of the basis to support a search warrant. He stated:

The information given by the anonymous informant was compelling in that it identified the location of the cultivation operation and located the appellant's house in a fairly specific geographic region, albeit without specifying an exact street address. It is impossible to determine whether the source was credible except by reference to the fact that the information was subsequently corroborated by a police reconnaissance which resulted in identification of the exact address of the residence described by the informant. The tip itself, therefore, was compelling enough in its specification of the place in which the offence was occurring for the police to readily locate the exact address of [Plant's] residence and corroborate the report of the informant. *I conclude that the anonymous tip, although made by an unknown informant, was sufficiently reliable to have formed part of the reasonable grounds asserted in the information to obtain the warrant* [emphasis added].

A CONCURRING OPINION

Justice McLachlin (as she then was) agreed with the result and much of the reasoning in *Plant*. Aside from the computer records, she would have found a sufficient basis to issue a search warrant. However, she would not have treated the computer records as public. They were, in her view, private. They gave rise to a reasonable expectation of *confidence.* Justice McLachlin wrote:

The question in each case is whether the evidence discloses a reasonable expectation that the information will be kept in confidence and restricted to the purposes for which it is given. Although I find the case of electricity consumption records close to the line, I have concluded that the evidence here discloses a sufficient expectation of privacy to require the police to obtain a warrant before eliciting the information. I conclude that the information was not public, since there is no evidence suggesting that this information was available to the public and the police obtained access only by reason of a special arrangement.

The records are capable of telling much about one's personal lifestyle, such as how many people lived in the house and what sort of activities were probably taking place there. The records tell a story about what is happening inside a private dwelling, the most private of places. I think that a reasonable person looking at these facts would conclude that the records should be used only for the purpose for which they were made — the delivery and billing of electricity — and not divulged to strangers without proper legal authorization [emphasis added].

The very reason the police wanted these records was to learn about [Plant's] personal lifestyle, i.e. the fact that he was growing marijuana. More generally, electricity consumption records may, as already noted, reveal how many people live in a house and much about what they do. While not as revealing as many types of records, they can disclose important personal information.

My colleague notes that the relationship between [Plant] and the electricity commission was not one of confidence. *It seems to me that the question is not so much whether the relationship is one of confidence, so much as whether the particular records disclose a reasonable expectation of confidence* [emphasis added].

My colleague states that the information was generally available to the public. This, with respect, does not accord with the evidence, which as noted, suggests that the records were not open to the public, and that the police were able to access them only by using a special computer number which they had been given in confidence. This is an important factor; *had I been able to conclude that the records were open to the public, I might well have concluded with my colleague that [Plant] had no expectation of privacy in the records* [emphasis added].

My colleague also argues that the place and manner in which the information was retrieved belie a reasonable expectation of privacy, emphasizing that the police did not have to intrude into "places ordinarily considered private" like a house or hotel room to get the information. But, again with respect, this begs the question. Computers may and should be private places, where the information they contain is subject to the legal protection arising from a reasonable expectation of privacy. Computers may contain a wealth of personal information. Depending on its character, that information may be as private as any found in a dwelling house or hotel room.

CHALLENGE QUESTION

A "THEORETICAL" POSSIBILITY

Overflight surveillance is a developing technology. There is a possibility that it may soon allow for views "inside" a building, as well as sensitivity maps of heat escaping from such structures.

Q. To what extent should a court consider realistic scientific developments of devices such as FLIR in determining whether a search has taken place within the meaning of section 8 of the Charter?

The Supreme Court left no doubt that it is the present capacity of a device such as FLIR which should be examined, not the scientific potential for enhanced use. It is not that the Court questioned what an emerging science may bring. Rather, the

Court seemed to emphasize that it is the "here and now" that should be examined. This, in turn, seems to mean that if, for example, FLIR should be enhanced by science, then *Tessling* would not be binding as to the facts. On the contrary, the Court would look to the facts of the enhanced technology and apply the principles set out in *Tessling*.

For the Court, Justice Binnie wrote in the Tessling case:

> Moreover, because I emphasize the informational aspect, my focus is on the quality of information that FLIR imaging can actually deliver, whereas Abella J.A. [as she then was], looking to safeguard the home, looked more to the "'theoretical capacity'" of the FLIR technology. For example, her reasons include the prediction that "'the nature of the intrusiveness is subtle but almost Orwellian in its theoretical capacity."
>
> In my view, with respect, the reasonableness line has to be determined by looking at the information generated by existing FLIR technology, and then evaluating its impact on a reasonable privacy interest. If, as expected, the capability of FLIR and other technologies will improve and the nature and quality of the information hereafter changes, it will be a different case, and the courts will have to deal with its privacy implications at that time in light of the facts as they then exist.... The question is: Does FLIR technology in fact intrude on the reasonable sphere of privacy of an individual?

PROTECTION BEYOND PRIVACY

Are there "interests" beyond privacy which section 8 of Charter will protect against unreasonable search and seizure? Justice Binnie cited with approval the opinion of Justice Dickson, as he then was, in *Hunter v. Southam Inc.*, [1984] 2 *Supreme Court of Canada Reports* 145, at p. 159, who said: "I would be wary of foreclosing the possibility that the right to be secure against unreasonable search and seizure might protect interests beyond the right of privacy, but for purposes of the present appeal I am satisfied that its protections go at least that far."

Justice Binnie, for his part, did not expand on the comment of Justice Dickson (who later became chief justice of the Supreme Court of Canada).

CHALLENGE QUESTION

SEARCH AND SEIZURE: GROW-OPS AND USE

Q. Suppose there is an unlawful search of a marijuana grow-op. Should the fact that the penalty for marijuana use is lesser than that relating to the use of other proscribed drugs have any bearing on whether the results of that unlawful search may be entered in evidence in a criminal proceeding?

Unlawfully obtained evidence may be admitted in a criminal proceeding if it meets the conditions of section 24 of the Charter which provides:

(1) Anyone whose rights or freedoms, as guaranteed by this Charter, have been

infringed or denied may apply to a court of competent jurisdiction to obtain such remedy as the court considers appropriate and just in the circumstances.

(2) Where, in proceedings under subsection (1), a court concludes that evidence was obtained in a manner that infringed or denied any rights or freedoms guaranteed by this Charter, the evidence shall be excluded if it is established that, having regard to all the circumstances, the admission of it would bring the administration of justice into disrepute.

It can be argued, as Justice Abella did in *Tessling* when she was a member of the Ontario Court of Appeal, that the evidence should be excluded. The reason: There is "public, judicial, and political recognition that marijuana is at the lower end of the hierarchy of harmful drugs." That is, the use of different kinds of prohibited drugs may have different levels of individual harm. Thus, excluding the unlawfully obtained evidence, Justice Abella concluded, would not result in any significant social cost, while its admission, in her view, would bring the administration of justice into disrepute.

In *Tessling*, Justice Binnie, speaking for the Supreme Court, commented on the seriousness of the alleged offence both as a factor bearing upon the reasonableness of the search (and that means the expectation of privacy), and the role of section 24(2) as to the admission of unlawfully acquired evidence. His conclusions, especially as to section 24(2) in general, are in line with Justice Abella. Justice Binnie wrote:

I do not think that [the seriousness of the offence] is a factor in determining whether the [accused] did or did not have a reasonable expectation of privacy in the heat distribution patterns on the outside of his house. Rather, *[the seriousness of the offence] may more logically arise at the stage the court considers whether a particular search was reasonable, or whether the evidence obtained by an unreasonable search may be admitted into evidence under s. 24(2) of the Charter* [emphasis added].

YOU BE THE JUDGE

THE CASE OF FLOATING GAMBLING

The case that follows is real. It deals with unseen searches, this time on the "inside" of the suspected unlawful enterprise.

THE FACTS

During the summer of 1984, Toronto police started an investigation to locate "floating" gaming houses which they deemed were "frequented by gamblers of Oriental extraction." As part of this probe, the police officers went to downtown hotels and asked their security officers to inform them of "anything unusual as to Orientals attending hotels."

A few months later, the security staff at a major downtown hotel contacted the police with information relating to the possible use of the hotel for illegal gaming. Police visited the hotel and the room where the claimed gambling took place. The occupants of the room had rearranged the furniture to form a long table suitable for gambling. In addition, on searching the garbage left by the occupants, the police found many slips of paper bearing Chinese characters. The slips bore the address and number of the hotel room, and the chief investigating officer was able to identify these as notices similar to some which he knew were distributed to potential Asian gamblers in various restaurants in Toronto's Chinatown.

The police checked the hotel register. It noted that Santiago Wong had booked this room for later in the same month. On the basis of their findings, the police concluded that the room booked by Wong might be used for illegal gambling. After determining that it would not be possible to see into the room from the roof of the other wing of the hotel, the officers in charge of the investigation concluded that only video surveillance would enable them to further their investigation by actually monitoring what happened in the room booked by Wong.

The police rejected the idea of using undercover officers. On the basis of past experience, they were certain that the gaming would be behind locked doors — by and for Asians alone. Since the identity of Asian police officers was well known in the community, the investigating officers believed it would be virtually impossible to infiltrate the gambling sessions with undercover operators.

Once it was determined that video surveillance was the only practical way of monitoring the room, the officers contacted the Metro Police Intelligence Branch and a Crown Counsel to discuss the possibility of obtaining a warrant.

These discussions left the police officers with the impression that it would not be possible to obtain judicial authorization to conduct the video surveillance. The investigators then decided to proceed without this authorization, and they installed a video camera in the drapery valence of the room registered to Wong. The camera had a lens about the size of the lead of a pencil and was attached to simultaneous recording equipment which the police monitored from an adjacent hotel room. The equipment was put in place with the permission and co-operation of the hotel management. (A warrant might have been possible for an audio tap.)

The police monitored the activities in the rooms on five separate occasions. These observations left no doubt that illegal gambling sessions were being held in the hotel suite. This surveillance culminated in an early morning raid. The police entered the room with a key provided by management and found a large group of Asian males in the suite. A search of these persons revealed numerous slips of the type seized in their earlier search of the room. Wong had profit lists, while debt lists were seized from some of the other occupants of the room. The police seized gambling paraphernalia and a large amount of money found on the gaming table.

Wong and ten other accused men were later charged with the offence of keeping a common gaming house. At trial, all the accused pleaded not guilty. The trial judge dismissed the charges against all the accused. He held that the video surveillance of the accused violated section 8 of the Charter, and he excluded the evidence obtained under section 24(2) of the Charter.

The Crown's appeal to the Ontario Court of Appeal against the acquittal of Wong and the others was allowed, and a new trial ordered. The Court of Appeal ruled that, on the facts of this case, Wong could not be said to have had a reasonable expectation of privacy. Accordingly, the Court of Appeal held, section 8 of the Charter had no application and the evidence of the video surveillance was therefore admissible.

THE ISSUES

- Is video surveillance to be treated the same as an audio tap, where the Supreme Court of Canada had stated that it can constitute a "search" within the meaning of section 8 of the Charter and that, under the Criminal Code, a warrant, on proper showing, can be obtained?
- Is the reasonable expectation of privacy to be determined on the basis of whether the accused is aware of the risk of electronic surveillance?
- Does the fact of illegal activity (gambling) influence whether the secret video surveillance was legal?
- Does the fact that Wong solicited strangers to attend the gambling sessions make the events "public"?
- Even if the searches and seizures by the police were unlawful, may the evidence coming from them be admitted in the criminal proceedings?

POINTS TO CONSIDER

- On a "regular basis," Wong had booked the room where the search and seizure occurred.
- The purpose in using the room was to conduct unlawful gambling and, toward that end,

people of "Oriental extraction" had been solicited through notices handed out in restaurants
in Toronto's Chinatown.

- The room searched was kept locked. Strangers
  were admitted only by permission.
- At the time of this case, the right of police under
  the Criminal Code to obtain a search warrant
  for taps related to audio surveillance.
- For purposes of conviction, police believed that
  video surveillance was the most effective form
  of surveillance.
- Section 8 of the Charter guarantees everyone
  "has the right to be secure against unreasonable
  search and seizure."
- Section 24(2) of the Charter provides: "Where
  ... a court concludes that evidence was obtained
  in a manner that infringed or denied any rights
  or freedoms guaranteed by this Charter, the
  evidence shall be excluded if it is established
  that, having regard to all the circumstances, the
  admission of it in the proceedings would bring
  the administration of justice into disrepute."

DISCUSSION

The facts are based largely on the Supreme Court of Canada
decision in *The Queen v. Wong*, [1990] 3 *Supreme Court
Reports* 36. There, a seven-member panel of the Court
allowed the evidence flowing from the search and seizure
to be received by the trial court.

The decision, however, brought three opinions,

including a dissent from Justice Wilson, who deemed the video surveillance unlawful and would have denied use of the results within the meaning of section 24(2) of the Charter. (Then) Chief Justice Antonio Lamer and Justice McLachlin agreed with the result of the majority. But, they did so on the basis that, in effect, no search took place. The gambling was treated as a public, not a private, matter. We will deal with each opinion in this discussion.

THE MAJORITY OPINION

Justice Gérard La Forest spoke for the Court majority of four. He emphasized that the right to privacy under section 8 of the Charter (protection against unreasonable search and seizure) is one "meant to keep pace with technological development and, accordingly, to ensure that we are ever protected against unauthorized intrusions upon our privacy by the agents of the state, whatever technical form the means of invasion may take." Thus, the Court's decision applied the rights under section 8 to video surveillance just as it had done to audio taps.

But a central question remained as to whether the gaming sessions themselves gave rise to a reasonable expectation of privacy. If there were such an expectation, then the accused was entitled to the rights under section 8 of the Charter. Justice La Forest rejected the arguments of the Crown, set out below, and sustained the claimed right to privacy.

RISK ANALYSIS

To what extent, if any, should a court inquire into whether an individual has "courted the risk of surveillance"? That is, should a court ask whether the accused has been aware that his activities, by their very nature (illegal gambling), might have been monitored by the police? The Court majority rejected the need for such an inquiry. Justice La Forest spoke initially of audio surveillance, and then the technology of video surveillance:

> When the intrusion takes the form of unauthorized and surreptitious electronic audio surveillance ... it [is] clear that to sanction such an intrusion would see our privacy diminished in just such an unacceptable manner. While there are societies in which persons have learned, to their cost, to expect that a microphone may be hidden in every wall, it is the hallmark of a society such as ours that its members hold to the belief that they are free to go about their daily business without running the risk that their words will be recorded at the sole discretion of agents of the state....
>
> I am firmly of the view that if a free and open society cannot brook the prospect that the agents of the state should, in the absence of judicial authorization, enjoy the right to record the words of whomever they choose, it is equally inconceivable that the state should have unrestricted discretion to target whomever it wishes for surreptitious video surveillance. George Orwell in his classic dystopian [an imaginary dehumanized and fearful place] novel *1984* paints

a grim picture of a society whose citizens had every reason to expect that their every movement was subject to electronic video surveillance. The contrast with the expectations of privacy in a free society such as our own could not be more striking. The notion that the agencies of the state should be at liberty to train hidden cameras on members of society wherever and whenever they wish is fundamentally irreconcilable with what we perceive to be acceptable behaviour on the part of government. As in the case of audio surveillance, to permit unrestricted video surveillance by agents of the state would seriously diminish the degree of privacy we can reasonably expect to enjoy in a free society.

UNLAWFUL ACTIVITY

The Court of Appeal, based on the facts, had ruled that neither Wong nor others attending the gambling sessions could have had any expectation of privacy. The very nature of the activity, said the Court of Appeal, was in a real sense public. After all, notices announcing the sessions had been distributed in a number of restaurants in Toronto's Chinatown. In effect, Justice La Forest said, the Court of Appeal had looked to the unlawful activity to determine whether there was any expectation of privacy on the part of Wong or others in attendance.

Justice La Forest said this was the wrong question and an inappropriate test for determining an expectation of privacy. He wrote:

It would be an error to suppose that the question that must be asked ... is whether persons who engage in illegal activity behind the locked door of a hotel room have a reasonable expectation of privacy. Rather, the question must be framed in broad and neutral terms so as to become whether in a society such as ours persons who retire to a hotel room and close the door behind them have a reasonable expectation of privacy.

Viewed in this light, it becomes obvious that the protections of section 8 of the Charter are meant to shield us from warrantless video surveillance when we occupy hotel rooms. Clearly, our homes are places in which we will be entitled, in virtually all conceivable circumstances, to affirm that unauthorized video surveillance by the state encroaches on a reasonable expectation of privacy. It would be passing strange if the situation should be any different in hotel or motel rooms. Normally, the very reason we rent such rooms is to obtain a private enclave where we may conduct our activities free of uninvited scrutiny. Accordingly, I can see no conceivable reason why we should be shorn of our right to be secure from unreasonable searches in these locations which may be aptly considered to be our homes away from home....

Nor, with respect, can I attach any importance to the fact that in the circumstances of this case [Wong] may have opened his door to strangers, or circulated invitations to the gaming sessions. I am simply unable to discern any logical nexus between these factors, and the conclusion that the police should have been free to videotape the proceedings in the hotel room at their sole discretion. It is safe to presume that a multitude of functions open to invited persons are held every week in hotel rooms across the country. These meetings will attract persons who share a common interest but who will often be strangers to each other. Clearly, persons who attend such meetings cannot expect their presence to go unnoticed by those in attendance. But, by the same token, it is no part of the reasonable expectations of those who hold or attend such gatherings that as a price of doing so they must tacitly consent to allowing agents of the state unfettered discretion to make a permanent electronic recording of the proceedings....

Were the reasonableness of unauthorized video surveillance to be gauged by the standard adopted by the Court of Appeal, the state would be at liberty to train its hidden cameras on an extremely broad spectrum of the activities engaged in by members of society. In effect, we would be debarred from asserting a reasonable expectation of freedom from clandestine electronic scrutiny on the part of the state at any private function to which members of the public had received an invitation.

Moreover, it is also clear that those ordinary measures which persons in a free and open society believe suffice to shut out uninvited scrutiny would be of no avail if the police (and they would of course be the sole arbiters of the matter) entertained the suspicion that the persons in the location concerned were involved in illegal activity. Here, it must be remembered that while [Wong] had rented a room in an establishment to which selected members of the public had access, he had seen to it that activities in the room were conducted behind locked doors and drawn drapes.

In effect, by application of the standard adopted by the Court of Appeal, members of society would be driven back to the confines of their homes if they wished to be sure of being able to escape the risk of unauthorized video surveillance. And even this ultimate refuge could be breached if the police formulated a suspicion with respect to gatherings in the home, for I think it must be conceded that on the reasoning of the Court of Appeal [Wong] could have asserted no reasonable expectation of privacy if the gambling sessions had been conducted in his own home.

CREATIVE READING OF SEARCH WARRANT AUTHORITY

The Criminal Code, at the time, allowed police to obtain a warrant to tap oral communications. Was it not possible, the Crown argued, for this authority to be expanded in a "creative" way to permit a warrant for video surveillance? If so, then, at most, what the police did was a technical violation, and their search should be deemed valid. The Court of Appeal rejected this argument; and so did Justice La Forest for a majority of the Supreme Court. Such expansion is a decision for Parliament to make, not the courts. He stated:

> Part IV.1 of the [Criminal] Code [which permits warrants for a wire tap of oral communications] is designed to set strict limits on the ability of the agents of the state to intercept private oral communications. It does not speak to the very different, and I might add, more pernicious threat to privacy constituted by surreptitious video surveillance. On my view of the matter, the courts would be forgetting their role as guardians of our fundamental liberties if they were to usurp the role of Parliament and purport to give their sanction to video surveillance by adapting for that purpose a code of procedure dealing with an altogether different surveillance technology.
>
> It is for Parliament, and Parliament alone, to set out the conditions under which law enforcement agencies may

employ video surveillance technology in their fight against crime. Moreover, the same holds true for any other technology which the progress of science places at the disposal of the state in the years to come. Until such time as Parliament, in its wisdom, specifically provides for a code of conduct for a particular invasive technology, the courts should forebear from crafting procedures authorizing the deployment of the technology in question. *The role of the courts should be limited to assessing the constitutionality of any legislation passed by Parliament which bears on the matter* [emphasis added].

SECTION 24(2) OF THE CHARTER

What the police carried out was an unlawful search and seizure within the meaning of section 8 of the Charter. But, that was not the end of the matter. There remained section 24(2) of the Charter, which would exclude the evidence from that search if to do so would "bring the administration of justice into disrepute."

Central to answering this question, Justice La Forest said, is the impact of receiving such evidence on the fairness of the trial. It is true, he continued, that the breach of section 8 did infringe an important right of privacy. Yet, the violation by the police was not intentional. They had sought the advice of Crown counsel in terms of whether a warrant might be obtained for video surveillance, and they received a negative response. In the police view, there was no real substitute for video surveillance. The breach of privacy was offset. He stated: "While the offence here is not, in itself, among the most serious in the Code, it is not beside the point that the proceeds from these offences were to be used to foster far more serious crimes.... In these circumstances, I would hold that [Wong] has not established that the admission of the evidence would bring the administration of justice into disrepute."

A CONCURRING OPINION

Chief Justice Lamer and Justice McLachlin, as they were then, concurred in the result of the majority, but not with the reasoning. They accepted that there is the expectation of privacy when one enters a hotel room. But the facts in *Wong* were different. The invitations to gamble were open to the public by notice, although in Chinese. The effect of this, the chief justice and Justice McLachlin stated, was that Wong could not have had any expectation of privacy. Thus, there was no search within the meaning of section 8 of the Charter. The result might have been different if fewer invitations had been extended. The concurring opinion stated:

> [Wong] was situated in a hotel room. In most cases, a hotel room is a location in which one has a reasonable expectation of privacy. However, in this case, [Wong] had, indiscriminately, extended invitations to the gaming session which was to take place in the hotel room. He had passed out numerous notices in public restaurants and bars, thereby inviting the public into

the hotel room. It is impossible to conclude that a reasonable person, in the position of [Wong], would expect privacy in these circumstances. A reasonable person would know that when such an invitation is extended to the public at large, one can no longer expect that strangers, including the police, will not be present in the room. In this case, the police effected their presence in the room via the video camera which was installed in the drapery valence.

I do not wish to be taken as adopting the risk analysis which this Court [had earlier] rejected.... I am not equating the risk that strangers will be in the hotel room with the risk that the police will be electronically recording the activity in the hotel room. The issue is not so much concerned with risk as it is with reasonable expectations. Here it was not reasonable for [Wong] to expect that strangers, including the police, would not be present in the room.

[Wong] may well have had a reasonable expectation of privacy in the hotel room had he extended a few invitations to particular individuals. However, that was not the case here. In my view, and with respect for other views, [Wong] had no reasonable expectation of privacy in these circumstances; as a result, no search took place within the meaning of section 8.

DISSENTING OPINION

Justice Wilson dissented. She would have denied use of the evidence obtained from the search within the meaning of section 24(2) of the Charter. Her reasons centred on: the seriousness of the unlawful search, and the lack of seriousness of the crime.

As to the first point, the police had two days' notice of the gambling sessions. They had other and lawful means to obtain evidence. For example, a warrant could have been sought for a wiretap. There was no showing that such a tap would have been considerably less effective than video surveillance. And, the police might have used informants — perhaps even the same informants who initially had told them of the sessions — to attend the gambling sessions. In the result, Justice Wilson stated, the unlawful use of video surveillance must be seen as intentional on the part of the police.

And, as to the second point, there was no real showing by the police that the offence of the floating gambling sessions either was a serious offence or gave rise to serious offences. She stated:

> The seriousness of the offence with which an accused is charged is particularly relevant in this regard. In this case, however, the police themselves, as I have noted above, did not consider the offence to be of a very serious nature. While it was suggested that the operation of gambling houses was sometimes accompanied by violence, no substantial evidence was led on this point. In the circumstances, given the type of evidence at issue in this appeal, the fact that

> the violation of the accused's Charter rights was serious because it was so unnecessary, and the fact that the offence with which the accused was charged was not in the very serious category, I conclude that the admission of the video tape evidence would tend to bring the administration of justice into repute and that it should be excluded.

POLICE PURSUING LEADS: INTERNET PROVIDERS

Can Internet providers give police the names and addresses of customers without court approval? This question was answered by a unanimous Supreme Court of Canada in *The Queen v. Matthew David Spencer*, 2014 *Supreme Court of Canada*.

Spencer was charged with the possession of child pornography and making it available through his computer. How Saskatoon police came to investigate him and, more particularly, focus on his computer and its files containing child pornography (which were apparently open to others) are facts key to the charges against him.

Central to Spencer's defence was his claim that the police search and seizure violated his Charter rights against unreasonable search and seizure.

THE FACTS
Spencer lived with his sister and connected to the Internet through an account in her name. He used the file sharing program LimeWire on his desktop computer to download child pornography.

LimeWire is a free peer-to-peer file sharing program that, at the time, anyone could download onto their computer. Peer-to-peer systems such as LimeWire allow users to download files directly from the computers of other users. LimeWire does not have one central database of files but, instead, relies on its users to share their files directly with others. It is commonly used to download music and movies and can also be used to download both adult and child pornography. It was Spencer's use of the file sharing software that brought him to the attention of the police and, ultimately, led to the search questioned in this case.

As part of his regular duty, Constable Darren Parisien of the Saskatoon Police Service, by using publicly available software, searched for anyone sharing child pornography. He could access whatever another user of the software had in his or her shared folder. In other words, he could "see" what other users of the file sharing software could "see." He could also obtain two numbers related to a given user: (1) the IP address that corresponds to the particular Internet connection through which a computer accesses the Internet at the time; and (2) the globally unique identifier (GUID) number assigned to each computer using particular software. The IP address of the computer from which shared material is obtained is displayed as part of the file sharing process.

For the purposes of this case, we know that the IP address obtained by Constable Parisien matched computer activity at the particular point in time of his investigation.

Constable Parisien generated a list of IP addresses for computers that had shared what he believed to be child pornography. He then ran that list of IP addresses against a database which matches IP addresses with approximate locations. He found that one of the IP addresses was suspected to be in Saskatoon, with Shaw Communications as the ISP (provider).

Constable Parisien then determined that Spencer's computer was online and connected to LimeWire. As a result, he (along with any LimeWire user) was able to browse the shared folder. When he did this, he saw an extensive amount of what he believed to be child pornography.

What Constable Parisien lacked was knowledge of where exactly the computer was located and who was using it. He got that information by making a "law enforcement request" to Shaw, the Internet provider. What he wanted was subscriber information as to the name, address, and telephone number of the person using the IP address.

The request was made under authority of a police claim of an ongoing investigation of child pornography in violation of the Criminal Code. The police argued that the "request" took the place of a search warrant.

Shaw complied with the request and provided the name, address, and telephone number of the customer associated with the IP address: Spencer's sister. With this information in hand, the police obtained a warrant to search Ms. Spencer's home (where Spencer lived) and seize Spencer's computer, which they did. The search of Spencer's computer revealed hundreds of child pornography images and over a hundred child pornography videos in his shared LimeWire folder.

Spencer was charged with possessing child pornography and making child pornography available over the internet contrary to section 163.1(3) of the Criminal Code. (There was no dispute that the images found in his shared folder were child pornography.)

At trial, Spencer asked to exclude evidence found on his computer. He said that the police were not likely to have found that evidence without being given his address by Shaw — an action taken without court approval. This action, said Spencer, amounted to unreasonable search and seizure under section 8 of the Charter.

The trial judge rejected Spencer's argument and convicted him of possession of child pornography. On appeal, the Saskatchewan Court of Appeal upheld the trial court decision with respect to the search issue.

THE SUPREME COURT OF CANADA DECIDES

The case then came on appeal to the Supreme Court of Canada. Justice Cromwell gave the decision for a unanimous Court. The Court ruled the police had indeed conducted a search, and that the search was unlawful. However, the Court said, the evidence obtained from the search might be introduced at Spencer's trial.

How could the Court find the search was unlawful and then allow the results of that search to be used at trial? Perhaps the best way to approach the Court's decision is to take it one step at a time. In point form, the reasoning of the Court follows:

1. The Court's reasoning centred on the facts of the case. It asked what the "significance" of the information was that the police wanted from the provider (Shaw). How could simply getting the name and address of a subscriber be an interest entitled to constitutional protection?

2. The answer is that the Court looks to all of the facts surrounding the police request — the "totality of the circumstances." One of these circumstances is the right to privacy.

3. To help us understand the nature of privacy, as applied to Spencer, the Court looked to "the thing being searched and the impact of the search on its target, not the legal or illegal nature of the items sought." Justice Cromwell said: "The issue is not whether Mr. Spencer had a legitimate interest in concealing his use of the Internet for the purpose of accessing child pornography, but whether people generally have a privacy interest in subscriber information with respect to computers which they use in their home for private purposes."

4. Another way of expressing "privacy" is to use the word "anonymity" which, said Justice Cromwell, is not a novel concept in the law. He wrote:

> The notion of privacy as anonymity is not novel. It appears in a wide array of contexts ranging from anonymous surveys to the protection of police informant identities. A person responding to a survey readily agrees to provide what may well be highly personal information. A police informant

provides information about the commission of a crime. The information itself is not private — it is communicated precisely so that it will be communicated to others. But the information is communicated on the basis that it will not be identified with the person providing it.

Consider situations in which the police want to obtain the list of names that correspond to the identification numbers on individual survey results or the defence in a criminal case wants to obtain the identity of the informant who has provided information that has been disclosed to the defence. The privacy interest at stake in these examples is not simply the individual's name, but the link between the identified individual and the personal information provided anonymously. As the intervener the Canadian Civil Liberties Association [in the Spencer case] urged in its submissions, "maintaining anonymity can be integral to ensuring privacy."

The mere fact that someone leaves the privacy of their home and enters a public space does not mean that the person abandons all of his or her privacy rights, despite the fact that as a practical matter, such a person may not be able to control who observes him or her in public. Thus, in order to uphold the protection of privacy rights in some contexts, we must recognize anonymity as one conception of privacy: see E. Paton-Simpson, "Privacy and the Reasonable Paranoid: The Protection of Privacy in Public Places" (2000), 50 University of Toronto Law Journal 305, at pp. 325–26.

5. Yet, isn't there a real danger in the scope that might be given to "anonymity" and "privacy" in impeding police

investigations, especially in terms of the Internet? In *Spencer*, Justice Cromwell said:

> The Internet has exponentially increased both the quality and quantity of information that is stored about Internet users. Browsing logs, for example, may provide detailed information about users' interests. Search engines may gather records of users' search terms.
>
> Advertisers may track their users across networks of websites, gathering an overview of their interests and concerns. "Cookies" may be used to track consumer habits and may provide information about the options selected within a website, which web pages were visited before and after the visit to the host website, and any other personal information provided: see N. Gleicher, "Neither a Customer Nor a Subscriber Be: Regulating the Release of User Information on the World Wide Web" (2009), 118 *Yale Law Journal* 1945, at pp. 194849; R. W. Hubbard, P. DeFreitas and S. Magotiaux, "The Internet – Expectations of Privacy in a New Context" (2002), 45 *Criminal Law Quarterly* 170, at pp. 189–91. The user cannot fully control or even necessarily be aware of who may observe a pattern of online activity, but by remaining anonymous — by guarding the link between the information and the identity of the person to whom it relates — the user can in large measure be assured that the activity remains private.

6. For these reasons, the Supreme Court said that the identity of a person linked to his/her use of the Internet does give rise to a privacy interest beyond that of the person's name,

address, and telephone number found in the subscriber information. For example, a police sniffer dog, by its trained reaction, can provide information about the contents of a bag and thus "engages ... privacy interests relating to its contents." Justice Cromwell wrote: "In the circumstances of this case [*Spencer*], the police request to link a given IP address to subscriber information was in effect a request to link a specific person (or a limited number of persons in the case of shared Internet services) to specific online activities. This sort of request engages the anonymity aspect of the informational privacy interest."

7. The fact that the police made a "request" for the information from the online provider, who then gave the information, did not convert that request into a "lawful demand." There was no lawful search warrant issued, for example, by a court for the subscriber information as to identity and address.

The end result, said Justice Cromwell, was that the search was unlawful.

BUT, WAS THAT THE END OF THE MATTER?

Was it possible that the results of even an unlawful search could still be used by the police, or by the Crown prosecutor?

Spencer's rights under the Charter were violated. But section 24(2) of the Charter allows for the admission of the questioned evidence unless doing so would bring "the administration of justice into disrepute."

Justice Cromwell listed three points that the Court considered, which led to the conclusion that keeping the evidence out rather than allowing it to be considered would bring the administration of justice into disrepute. He wrote:

> The court must assess and balance the effect of admitting the evidence on society's confidence in the justice system having regard to: (1) the seriousness of the Charter-infringing state conduct ... (2) the impact of the breach on the Charter-protected interests of the accused ... and (3) society's interest in the adjudication of the case on its merits.
>
> Turning first to the seriousness of the state conduct, my view is that it cannot be characterized as constituting either "wilful or flagrant disregard of the Charter." The investigating constable testified that he believed the request to Shaw was authorized by law and that Shaw could consent to provide the information to him. He also testified, however, that he was aware that there were decisions both ways on the issue of whether this was a legally acceptable practice.

While Justice Cromwell did not want to be understood to be encouraging the police to act without warrants in "gray areas," his belief was clearly reasonable in light of the fact that the trial judge and three judges of the Court of Appeal concluded that the constable had acted lawfully. In short, the police were acting by what they reasonably thought were lawful means to pursue an important law enforcement purpose. The nature of the police conduct in this case would not tend to bring the administration of justice into disrepute.

The second factor is the impact of the Charter-infringing conduct on Spencer's Charter-protected interests. That impact here was serious. As discussed above, anonymity is an important safeguard for privacy interests online. The violation of that anonymity exposed personal choices made by Spencer to be his own, and subjected them to police scrutiny as such. This weighed in favour of excluding the evidence.

That brought Justice Cromwell to the final factor: society's interest in an adjudication on the merits. While the public has a heightened interest in seeing a determination on the merits where the offence charged is serious, it also has a vital interest in having a justice system that is above reproach, particularly where the penal stakes for the accused are high. Justice Cromwell concluded:

> The offences here are serious and carry minimum prison sentences. Society has both a strong interest in the adjudication of the case and also in ensuring that the justice system remains above reproach in its treatment of those charged with these serious offences. If the evidence is excluded, the Crown will effectively have no case. The impugned evidence (the electronic files containing child pornography) is reliable and was admitted by the defence at trial to constitute child pornography. Society undoubtedly has an interest in seeing a full and fair trial based on reliable evidence, and all the more so for a crime which implicates the safety of children.
>
> Balancing the three factors, my view is that exclusion of the evidence rather than its admission would bring the administration of justice into disrepute, and I would uphold its admission.

The Supreme Court of Canada sent the case back for a new trial on the issue of whether Spencer had made the photographs available to others — a separate charge. The question bore directly on computers and the Internet.

No one suggested that Spencer, in fact, handed the pictures over to any person. Rather, the Crown took the position that he was wilfully blind to the potential use of the files.

Citing another Supreme Court decision, Justice Cromwell said: "A finding of wilful blindness involves an affirmative answer to the question: Did the accused shut his eyes because he knew or strongly suspected that looking would fix him with knowledge [i.e. intent]?"

EDITORIAL COMMENT

The *Globe and Mail* made the following editorial comment on *The Queen v. Matthew David Spencer*:

> The Supreme Court was right on Friday to reassert the search-warrant principle in the electronic age. Customers of an Internet service provider, said the court, have a reasonable expectation that their subscriber information for an IP address will be private. Companies should not blithely and routinely hand it over to the police, without a judicial authorization.
>
> In this case, Shaw Communications Inc. voluntarily gave a police officer such information about a suspected — and as it turned out, actual — collector of child pornography, Matthew Spencer. Constable Darren Parisien knew there was some doubt about whether a warrant was needed, but he acted in good faith. And once he identified the suspect's house, he quite properly obtained a search warrant to enter the house.
>
> The federal government's Bill C-13, the misnamed Protecting Canadians from Online Crime Act, if it is passed, would confirm the warrant requirement. Under C-13, a police officer applying for judicial authorization of access to the subscriber information for the IP address would

presumably face the lesser threshold of "reasonable suspicion," rather than the more demanding standard of reasonable and probable grounds for a search warrant. Either way, they'd have to show evidence and seek the approval of a judge.

Over the past few months, Canadians have been treated to a growing barrage of stories about the ways in which agencies of government are able to get extralegal access to information about Canadians' phone and e-mail accounts. The court reminded us that this is at odds with our most fundamental constitutional principles. For government to access your private information, a judge's authorization should normally be required (*Globe and Mail*, June 15, 2014).

REFERENCES AND FURTHER READING

* Cited by the Supreme Court of Canada.

Amsterdam, Anthony G. "Perspectives on the Fourth Amendment." *Minnesota Law Review* 58 (1974): 349.*

Blanchfield, Mike. "Online Privacy: Supreme Court Says Warrant Needed for Internet Info." *huffingtonpost.ca*, June 13, 2014.

———. "Big Marijuana Factory Was One Strange Joint." *Globe and Mail*, January 13, 2004.

Cheney, Peter. "The Massive Secret Inside Barrie's Former Brewery." *Globe and Mail*, January 12, 2004.

Fine, Sean. "Online Anonymity Ruled as Vital." *Globe and Mail*, June 14, 2014.

Freeze, Colin, and Dawn Walton. "Drug Crime Nourished in Sleepy Communities." *Globe and Mail*, March 5, 2005.

"Get a Warrant If You Want to Get Into an IP Address." *Globe and Mail,* June 16, 2014.

Gleicher, Nathaniel. "Neither a Customer Nor a Subscriber Be: Regulating the Release of User Information on the World Wide Web." *Yale Law Journal* 118 (2009): 1945.*

Gutterman, Melvin. "A Formulation of the Value and Means Models of the Fourth Amendment in the Age of Technologically Enhanced Surveillance." *Syracuse Law Review* 39 (1988): 647.

Ha, Tu Thanh. "Predators and Privacy: Ruling Set to Stoke Debate on Police's Telecom Ties." *Globe and Mail,* June 12, 2014.

Hubbard, Robert, et al. "The Internet – Expectations of Privacy in New Context." *Criminal Law Quarterly* 45 (2009): 170.

Hume, Mark. "Police Can't Keep Up with Growth of Pot Farms, Study Finds." *Globe and Mail,* March 11, 2005.

Orwell, George. *Nineteen Eighty-Four.* Toronto: Penguin Books, 1949.*

Paton-Simpson, Elizabeth. "Privacy and the Reasonable Paranoid: The Protection of Privacy in Public Places." *University of Toronto Law Journal* 50 (200): 305.

Presser, Jill. "Here's to Privacy in Your Online Life." *Globe and Mail,* June 17, 2014.

Report of a Task Force established jointly by Department of Communications/Department of Justice. *Privacy and Computers.* Information Canada, Ottawa, 1972.*

Rosenthal, Andrew. "The House Actually Did Something About Warrantless Surveillance." *New York Times,* June 20, 2014.

Slane Andrea, and Lisa M. Austin. "What's in a Name? Privacy and Citizenship in the Voluntary Disclosure of Subscriber Information in Online Child Exploitation Investigations." *Criminal Law Quarterly* 57 (2011).*

"The Pot Law May Stand, But It Still Needs Fixing." *Globe and Mail,* January 2, 2004.

Westin, Alan F. *Privacy and Freedom.* Atheneum, NY: 1970.*

CHAPTER 3

STOP-AND-FRISK AND PAT-DOWN

By what right may police stop those simply walking in public places? Assume that police have no grounds for believing that such persons have committed any offence. Now, further assume that the police not only stop, but they politely but firmly frisk and pat-down (feeling the outside of a person's clothing) the individual stopped — much like airport security clearances. Finally, assume that in the pat-down police find illegal drugs. May the drugs found be evidence to support criminal charges? This is the subject matter of this chapter.

Among the questions raised in this chapter are:

- What are police "stop-and-frisk" and "pat-down" searches?
- What limits does the Charter place on such searches?
- Can police ever conduct an otherwise unlawful search?
- Is it possible for the evidence of an unlawful search to be used in a later criminal proceeding?

Section 10 of the Charter of Rights and Freedoms provides: "Everyone has the right on arrest or detention (a) to be informed promptly of the reasons therefor; (b) to retain and instruct counsel without delay and to be informed of that right...." Note that the Charter speaks of both arrest and detention. A central question is whether a pat-down requires police to promptly inform the individual of the reasons for the action, and then to afford that individual the opportunity to obtain a lawyer.

The main case for discussion in this chapter is *The Queen v. Mann and the Attorney General of Ontario, the Canadian Association of Chiefs of Police, the Criminal Lawyers' Association (Ontario) and the Canadian Civil Liberties Association (Interveners)*, decided by the Supreme Court of Canada on July 23, 2004. This was a 5–2 decision with the majority opinion handed down by Justice Frank Iacobucci and the dissent by Justice Michel Bastarache, who was joined by Justice Deschamps.

We will find that while there are general rules for police to follow in stop-and-frisk matters, the detailed law is worked out in the facts of individual cases. Justice Iacobucci, for the majority in *The Queen v. Mann*, wrote:

> This appeal presents fundamental issues on the right of individuals to walk the streets free from state interference, but in recognition of the necessary role of the police in criminal investigation. As such, this case offers another opportunity to consider the delicate balance that must be struck in adequately protecting individual liberties and properly recognizing legitimate police functions....
>
> Nowhere do these interests collide more frequently than in the area of criminal investigation. Charter rights do not exist in a vacuum; they are animated at virtually every stage of police action. Given their mandate to investigate crime and keep the peace, police officers must be empowered to respond quickly, effectively, and flexibly to the diversity of encounters experienced daily on

the front lines of policing. Despite there being no formal consensus about the existence of a police power to detain for investigative purposes, several commentators note its long-standing use in Canadian policing practice.

We will present the facts and then the analysis given by the majority in *The Queen v. Mann*. Some reference will be made to U.S. Supreme Court cases. The reason is that such cases were noted and discussed by the Supreme Court of Canada in the Mann case. In part, the Supreme Court of Canada did this because the U.S. cases arose under that part of the U.S. Constitution — namely, the Fourth Amendment of the Bill of Rights — prohibiting unreasonable search or seizure, a provision similar to section 8 of the Charter which provides: "Everyone has the right to be secure against unreasonable search or seizure."

There is another important area for discussion arising from pat-down cases: How should evidence seized in an unlawful pat-down be treated? Should the Crown be permitted to introduce such evidence in a criminal proceeding? These were the primary questions addressed by the dissent of Justice Bastarache in *The Queen v. Mann*. To answer these questions, the Court had to interpret section 24 of the Charter which provides:

> (1) Anyone whose rights or freedoms, as guaranteed by this Charter, have been infringed or denied may apply to a court of competent jurisdiction to obtain such remedy as the court considers appropriate and just in the circumstances.
>
> (2) Where, in proceedings under subsection (1), a court concludes that evidence was obtained in manner that infringed or denied any rights or freedoms guaranteed by this Charter, the evidence shall be excluded if it is established that, having

regard to all the circumstances, the admission of it in proceedings would bring the administration of justice into disrepute.

Note that section 24(2) does not require that the evidence coming from an unlawful search, in itself, be excluded from a later criminal proceeding. Rather, such evidence is to be excluded only "if it is established that, having regard to all the circumstances, the admission of it in proceedings would bring the administration of justice into disrepute." The meaning of this requirement was discussed both by the majority and dissent in *The Queen v. Mann*.

THE FACTS OF *THE QUEEN V. MANN*

On December 23, 2000, shortly before midnight, two police officers on duty together received a radio dispatch stating that a break and enter of a store was in progress. The location, a high-crime area in downtown Winnipeg, was close by. The dispatcher described a suspect in the break-in as a twenty-one-year-old aboriginal male, about five feet, eight inches tall, weighing about 165 pounds, and wearing a black jacket with white sleeves. The dispatcher said the suspect was thought to be Zachary Parisienne.

When the officers were within two blocks of the scene of the reported crime, they saw an individual "walking casually along the sidewalk." Each officer later testified that the person they saw matched the radio description "to the tee." They stopped the person — Philip Mann — and asked him to identify himself. Mann did so, giving his name and date of birth.

That was not enough for the police. They told Mann that they wanted to do a pat-down search for concealed weapons. The Supreme Court operated on the assumption that Mann gave his consent for such a search. This is what happened:

Mann was wearing a pullover sweater with a kangaroo pouch pocket in the front. The pat-down, in the view of the officers, did not result in any suspicion that Mann had a concealed weapon. However, during the pat-down, one officer felt a soft object in the pouch pocket. Again, the officer was certain that the object was not a weapon. But, in the officer's words, he was "curious." He slipped his hand inside the pocket and pulled out a small plastic bag containing 27.55 grams of marijuana. From another pocket, again acting on "curiosity," the officer pulled out a number of small plastic baggies, two Valium pills, and a treaty status card confirming Mann's identity.

After the pat-down, Mann was arrested. He was cautioned in terms of his right to a lawyer and his right to remain silent. The charge against him was possession for the purpose of trafficking in marijuana, contrary to section 5(2) of the Controlled Drugs and Substances Act.

The trial was held in a Manitoba provincial court. There, the judge ruled that the police did a pat-down of Mann "for security reasons." But, said the judge, there was no justification for the police to reach inside Mann's pocket after feeling a soft item. The police did not claim that they had any reason to be threatened by a concealed weapon — and there was no basis for finding one.

THE LOWER COURT DECISIONS

The provincial court judge concluded that the pat-down was an "unreasonable search" within the meaning of section 8 of the Charter which, as noted, guarantees that everyone has the right to be secure against unreasonable search and seizure. Further, the judge stated that the marijuana and baggies seized should not be received in evidence because, under section 24(2) of the Charter, to do so would interfere with the fairness of the trial. The result: Mann was acquitted.

The Crown appealed the provincial court decision to the Manitoba Court of Appeal which set aside the provincial court judgment. The Court of Appeal stated that the pat-down was both authorized by law and, based on the facts, reasonable. Initially, the Court of Appeal stated that the Crown had the burden of demonstrating the reasonableness of the search. This, said the Court of Appeal, was done. What the police did, the Court of Appeal stated, was within their duties as law enforcement officers in terms of "preserving the peace and protecting life." The officers only acted after they had established the likeness between Mann and the described suspect.

The Court of Appeal judgment as to the reasonableness of the police pat-down was based "on the good faith conduct of the officers in carrying out the protective search." For the court, looking at the matter, it was not reasonable for the police to look inside Mann's pouch after the pat-down disclosed no likelihood of a concealed weapon.

Still, the Court of Appeal stated that it was: "wary of placing too rigid a constraint on officers' ability to ensure a safe environment. [Police] officers should be allowed some latitude in this regard so long as the search was conducted in good faith. As the good faith conduct of the officers was unquestioned, the scope of the search had been reasonable in this case and there was no breach of [Mann's] right to be secure against unreasonable search and seizure under section 8 of the Charter."

THE SUPREME COURT DECIDES

All members of the Supreme Court of Canada agreed that the search of Mann resulting in his arrest was unlawful. Justice Iacobucci, for the Court majority, outlined the principles and then applied them to the facts. He did this recognizing that it is the trial court which should decide questions of fact. And, it is the appellate court — and, in this instance, the Supreme Court — which is the final determiner of the law. Justice Iacobucci stated:

> The case law raises several guiding principles governing the use of a police power to detain for

investigative purposes. The evolution of [that law] calls for investigative detentions to be premised upon reasonable grounds. The detention must be viewed as reasonably necessary on an objective view of the totality of the circumstances, informing the officer's suspicion that there is a clear nexus between the individual to be detained and a recent or ongoing criminal offence.

Reasonable grounds figures at the front-end of such an assessment, underlying the officer's reasonable suspicion that the particular individual is implicated in the criminal activity under investigation. The overall reasonableness of the decision to detain, however, must further be assessed against all of the circumstances, most notably the extent to which the interference with individual liberty is necessary to perform the officer's duty, the liberty interfered with, and the nature and extent of that interference....

Police powers and police duties are not necessarily correlative. While the police have a common law duty to investigate crime, they are not empowered to undertake any and all action in the exercise of that duty. Individual liberty interests are fundamental to the Canadian constitutional order. Consequently, any intrusion upon them must not be taken lightly and, as a result, police officers do not have *carte blanche* to detain. The power to detain cannot be exercised on the basis of a hunch, nor can it become a *de facto* arrest.

Any search incidental to the limited police power of investigative detention described above is necessarily a warrantless search. Such searches are presumed to be unreasonable unless they can be justified, and hence found reasonable.... Warrantless searches are deemed reasonable if (a) they are authorized by law, (b) the law itself is reasonable, and (c) the manner in which the search was carried out was also reasonable.... The Crown bears the burden of demonstrating, on the balance of probabilities, that the warrantless search was authorized by a reasonable law and carried out in a reasonable manner.

The Mann case was the first time the Court discussed whether a search flowing from an investigative detention is allowed by law. (But, as we shall see in other somewhat similar cases — such as investigative searches flowing from 911 hang-ups and roadblocks — the Court has allowed their use.) Justice Iacobucci said that the Court's analysis reflected the need to balance the competing interests of an individual's reasonable expectation of privacy with the interests of police officer safety. In doing this, he emphasized that police cannot use the limited exceptions of investigative detention to protect life or immediate crime investigation as a substitute for the constitutional obligation to obtain search warrants from a judicial officer on a showing of reasonable and probable cause. He wrote:

> In the context of an arrest, this Court has held that, in the absence of a warrant, police officers are empowered to search for weapons or to preserve evidence.... *I note at the outset the importance of maintaining a distinction between search incidental to arrest and search incidental to an investigative detention. The latter does not give license to officers to reap the seeds of a warrantless search without the need to effect a lawful arrest based on reasonable and probable grounds, nor does it erode the obligation to obtain search warrants where possible* [emphasis added].

[To be lawful] the search must be reasonably necessary. The relevant considerations here include the duty being performed, the extent to which some interference with individual liberty is necessary in the performance of that duty, the importance of the performance of the duty to the public good, the nature of the liberty being interfered with, and the nature and extent of the interference....

The general duty of officers to protect life may, in some circumstances, give rise to the power to conduct a pat-down search incident to an investigative detention. Such a search power does not exist as a matter of course; the officer must believe on reasonable grounds that his or her own safety, or the safety of others, is at risk.... The officer's decision to search must also be reasonably necessary in light of the totality of the circumstances. It cannot be justified on the basis of a vague or non-existent concern for safety, nor can the search be premised upon hunches or mere intuition.

PRINCIPLES APPLIED

Justice Iacobucci next spoke of the daily realities facing police. It was in such a context that the principles he outlined were to be applied:

Police officers face any number of risks every day in the carrying out of their policing function, and are entitled to go about their work secure in the knowledge that risks are minimized to the greatest extent possible. A frisk search is a "relatively non-intrusive procedure," the duration of which is "only a few seconds." Where an officer has reasonable grounds to believe that his or her safety is at risk, the officer may engage in a protective pat-down search of the detained individual. The search must be grounded in objective ... facts to prevent "fishing expeditions" on the basis of irrelevant or discriminatory factors.

Police officers may detain an individual for investigative purposes if there are reasonable grounds to suspect in all the circumstances that the individual is connected to a particular crime and that such a detention is necessary.

In addition, where a police officer has reasonable grounds to believe that his or her safety or that of others is at risk, the officer may engage in a protective pat-down search of the detained individual. Both the detention and the pat-down search must be conducted in a reasonable manner.... The investigative detention and protective search power are to be distinguished from an arrest and the incidental power to search on arrest, which do not arise in this case.

The officers had reasonable grounds to detain [Mann]. He closely matched the description of the suspect given by radio dispatch, and was only two or three blocks from the scene of the reported crime. These factors led the officers to reasonably suspect that [Mann] was involved in recent criminal activity, and at the very least ought to be investigated further. The presence of an individual in a so-called high crime area is relevant only so far as it reflects his or her proximity to a particular crime. The high crime nature of a neighbourhood is not by itself a basis for detaining individuals.

Furthermore, there were reasonable grounds for a protective search of [Mann]. There was a logical possibility that [Mann], suspected on reasonable grounds of having recently committed a break-and-enter, was in possession of break-and-enter tools, which could be used as weapons. The encounter also occurred just after midnight and there were no other people in the area. On balance, the officer was justified in conducting a pat-down search for protective purposes.

The officer's decision to go beyond this initial pat-down and reach into [Mann's] pocket after feeling an admittedly soft object therein is problematic. The trial judge found that the officer had no reasonable basis for reaching into the pocket. This more intrusive part of the search was an unreasonable violation of the [Mann's] reasonable expectation of privacy in the contents of his pockets.

The finding of the trial court that the police had no reason to go beyond the pat-down for the purpose of self-protection was one of fact. As such, it was binding on the appellate courts unless there were special circumstances calling for a different conclusion. Here there were not. The officer who reached into Mann's pocket said he did so to satisfy his curiosity, nothing more. Accordingly, Justice Iacobucci, for the Court, ruled the search yielding the drugs was unlawful (*Globe and Mail,* July 24, 2004).

PAT-DOWN QUESTIONING

Suppose, beyond asking for identification, police had questioned Mann during the pat-down. They wanted to know what "business" he had in the area. Indeed, they asked for an explanation as to why he was in Winnipeg. The questioning was not threatening, as such. Was Mann obligated to answer the police questions as part of a pat-down search? No. Justice Iacobucci, for the Court majority, stated: "I note that the investigative detention [pat-down] should be brief and it *does not impose an obligation on the detained individual to answer questions posed by the police*" [emphasis added].

A pat-down, it must be emphasized, is not an arrest which may have with it the power to search.

CHALLENGE QUESTIONS

A ROLE FOR PARLIAMENT?

In *The Queen v. Mann*, the Supreme Court of Canada set out certain rules as to when a pat-down would be permitted, and when the evidence obtained from such a search could be received in any later criminal trial.

For example, the Court clearly said that if the police had reason to believe their safety was at risk, a pat-down could take place. And, if in feeling the suspect's clothes a weapon were found, it could be taken. Charges could be laid, and the weapon could be received in evidence.

Such a rule, however, was not a law enacted by Parliament. Rather, it is the result of common law development by the courts. This means that, over the years, through decisions, the courts have established their own rules as to when a search and, more particularly, a pat-down will be lawful.

Q. Does Parliament have the power to enact laws that would set more precise boundaries for determining when a pat-down would be lawful? And, would such laws override the common law rules of the courts?

Yes, to both questions. But the answers are nuanced. Parliament does have the power to enact laws setting rules as to how searches, such as pat-downs, are to be carried out by police (or other law enforcement officers). However, such rules must comport with the Charter. And, in the final analysis, it is for the courts, and especially the Supreme Court of Canada, to interpret the law and find the facts in any case. Because Parliament has this power, the Court in *The Queen v. Mann* stated that it must tread carefully.

Justice Iacobucci, for the Court, wrote:

> At the same time, this Court must tread softly where complex legal developments are best left to the experience and expertise of legislators.... Major changes requiring the development of subsidiary rules and procedures relevant to their implementation are better accomplished through legislative deliberation than by judicial decree. It is for that very reason that I do not believe it appropriate for this Court to recognize a general power of detention for investigative purposes.
>
> The Court cannot, however, shy away from the task where common law rules are required to be incrementally adapted to reflect societal change. Courts, as its custodians, share responsibility for ensuring that the common law reflects current and emerging societal needs and values.... Here, our

duty is to lay down the common law governing police powers of investigative detention in the particular context of this case.

Where, as in this case, the relevant common law rule has evolved gradually through jurisprudential treatment [individual cases], the judiciary is the proper forum for the recognition and ordering of further legal developments, absent legislative intervention. Over time, the common law has moved cautiously to carve out a limited sphere for state intrusions on individual liberties in the context of policing.

The recognition of a limited police power of investigative detention marks another step in that measured development. It is, of course, open to Parliament to enact legislation in line with what it deems the best approach to the matter, subject to overarching requirements of constitutional compliance. As well, Parliament may seek to legislate appropriate practice and procedural techniques to ensure that respect for individual liberty is adequately balanced against the interest of officer safety. In the meantime, however, the unregulated use of investigative detentions in policing, their uncertain legal status, and the potential for abuse inherent in such low-visibility exercises of discretionary power are all pressing reasons why the Court must exercise its custodial role.

YOU BE THE JUDGE

A MATTER OF INTEREST?

THE FACTS

On a November evening in 2003, two police officers in downtown Vancouver (in a high-crime area known for the sale of drugs, especially crack cocaine) approached a small apartment building, long designated by police as a crack house. On numerous occasions, the police had obtained search warrants and made drug arrests, many of which had resulted in convictions.

On this evening, the officers saw Jason Edwards leaving the apartment building. Edwards began walking in the direction of the police squad car. The officers testified that when he spotted the car and made eye contact with them, he halted "abruptly, turned, and then moved in the opposite direction, going into a nearby alley." The officers believed that Edwards's movements were "evasive." They decided to investigate further.

They moved their squad car to the alley, found Edwards, and ordered him to stop and submit to a pat-down search. There was no appearance that Edwards carried a concealed weapon. However, the officer doing the search testified that he took an "interest" in a small lump in Edwards's nylon jacket. He testified: "As I pat-searched the front of [Edwards's] body, I felt a lump, a small lump, in the front pocket. I examined it with my fingers and it slid.... It felt [like] a lump of crack cocaine in cellophane."

The officer then reached into Edwards's pocket and took out a small plastic bag containing one-fifth of a gram of crack cocaine. Edwards was promptly arrested and charged with possession of a controlled substance. At trial, his counsel asked the court to suppress evidence of the cocaine.

THE ISSUES

- Were the officers justified in the pat-down search of Edwards to ensure that he was not carrying a concealed weapon?
- Were the officers justified in pulling the bag of cocaine from his jacket pocket as part of the pat-down search?

POINTS TO CONSIDER

- Section 8 of the Charter provides: "Everyone has the right to be secure against unreasonable search and seizure."
- A search ordinarily requires a warrant from a judicial officer describing with some precision what and where and when the search is to take place. And, a warrant is not issued unless the police (or Crown) are able to convince the magistrate that there is probable cause to believe it is necessary to a criminal investigation.
- A pat-down search is one where an officer detains a person for a short period of time in the conduct of a criminal investigation. The officer

feels the outside of the person's clothing, usually to determine if a weapon is being carried.

- The Supreme Court of Canada has ruled that police officers may conduct pat-down searches if there is a reasonable basis for believing they may be necessary to protect themselves or others. In this regard, it must be emphasized that such searches are designed for protection and not for criminal investigation.

- Yet, such pat-down searches may result in finding evidence of wrongdoing, such as possession of unlawful drugs which can be seized and used at a later trial. This can be done if police are lawfully in a position to view the object, and if its incriminating character is immediately apparent. Thus, if an officer lawfully pats down a suspect's outer clothing and feels an object whose contour or mass makes its identity immediately apparent, there has been no invasion of the suspect's privacy beyond that already authorized by the officer's search for weapons.

DISCUSSION

The pat-down search for the purpose of determining whether Edwards had a concealed weapon was lawful in terms of the police protecting themselves. Edwards was in an area where drugs were sold. Indeed, he had come from a place known to police as a crack house. But, the cocaine found as a result of the pat-down will be ruled the product of an unlawful search.

In *The Queen v. Mann,* Justice Iacobucci, speaking for the majority, referred to facts essentially the same as those set out here. They came from a decision of the U.S. Supreme Court: *Minnesota v. Dickerson,* 508 *United States Supreme Court Reports* [1993].

Justice Iacobucci found the U.S. law relevant. The reason: The Fourth Amendment of the U.S. Constitution is written in language strikingly similar to section 8 of the Charter: It prohibits unreasonable searches and seizures. And, the Constitution is the supreme law of the United States.

THE DECISION

In the Dickerson case, Justice Byron White, for the Court, ruled that the police had overstepped what was permitted *under the circumstances.* The Court majority stated that the police were permitted to do a pat-down for the purpose of protecting themselves — to ensure that the suspect had no concealed weapons. There was no reasonable basis for believing that the package was a weapon. Nor did it follow that the feel of the package necessarily implied that it was an unlawful drug. Justice White stated:

> The question before this Court is whether the officer who conducted the search was acting within the lawful bounds ... at the time he gained probable cause to believe that the lump in the defendant's jacket was contraband. The State [trial court] did not make precise findings on this point, instead finding simply that the officer, after feeling "a small, hard object

wrapped in plastic" in [the defendant's] pocket, "formed the opinion that the object ... was crack cocaine." The [trial] Court also noted that the officer made "no claim that he suspected this object to be a weapon" ... (The officer "never thought the lump was a weapon"). The Minnesota Supreme Court, after "a close examination of the record," held that the officer's own testimony belied any notion that he "immediately" recognized the lump as crack cocaine.... Rather, the court concluded, the officer determined that the lump was contraband only after "squeezing, sliding and otherwise manipulating the contents of the defendant's pocket" — a pocket which the officer already knew contained no weapon.

Under the State Supreme Court's interpretation of the record before it, it is clear that the court was correct in holding that the police officer in this case overstepped the bounds of the "strictly circumscribed" search for weapons.... Where, as here, "an officer who is executing a valid search for one item seizes a different item," this Court rightly "has been sensitive to the danger ... that officers will enlarge a specific authorization, furnished by a warrant or an [otherwise lawful pat-down], into the equivalent of a general warrant to rummage and seize at will." Here, the officer's continued exploration of [the defendant's] pocket after having concluded that it contained no weapon was unrelated to "the sole justification of the search ... the protection of the police officer and others nearby." It therefore amounted to the sort of evidentiary search that [this Court has] expressly refused to authorize, ... and that we have condemned in [other] cases....

Although the [searching] officer was lawfully in a position to feel the lump in [the defendant's jacket] pocket, ... the court below determined that the incriminating character of the object was not immediately apparent to him. Rather, the officer determined that the item was contraband only after conducting a further search, one not authorized by [law].... Because this further search of [the defendant's] pocket was constitutionally invalid, the seizure of the cocaine that followed is likewise unconstitutional.

The U.S. Supreme Court suppressed evidence of the cocaine seized in the pat-down. The defendant was acquitted.

YOU BE THE JUDGE

ROADBLOCKS AND SEARCHES WITHOUT WARRANTS

THE FACTS

A Quebec business was robbed. A description of the three robbers and their getaway vehicle (a pickup truck) was given to police. Within a short time, police established a roadblock. Vehicles and individuals similar to those described were pulled over to be questioned and, if the police believed it necessary, searched. In this regard, police also stopped vehicles similar to that described even if they appeared to contain only a driver. They believed that the other suspects might be hidden.

A pickup truck was pulled over at the roadblock. It matched the description given police. A taut piece of canvas blocked the truck's cargo area. Police thought the suspects might be hiding underneath it. The officers removed the canvas and discovered a quantity of smuggled cigarettes. Charges were laid. The defendant moved to have the evidence suppressed.

THE ISSUE

Was the police search of the pickup truck cargo area lawful?

POINTS TO CONSIDER

- The police had no precise description of the robbers.

- While the driver of the pickup truck was suspect, the police had no basis for holding him. Whether he would have been arrested depended on finding the other suspects in the truck.
- Looking at the canvas, itself, did not allow the police to conclude that any offence had been committed. It was only after they looked under the canvas that the unlawful cargo of cigarettes was found.
- In *The Queen v. Mann,* the Supreme Court of Canada stated that stop-and-frisk searches could take place where police had a reasonable basis for believe that a crime had taken place.
- The police did not stop the pickup truck because they had any reason for believing their safety was at risk.

DISCUSSION

The court allowed the police to make the search, and permitted the cigarettes they uncovered to be placed in evidence in support of the charges laid.

The facts come from a case before the Quebec Court of Appeal (*The Queen v. Murray,* [1999] 136 *Canadian Criminal Cases* (3rd series) 197) which was favourably cited both by the majority and dissent in *The Queen v. Mann.* The decision in the Quebec case was handed down by Fish, J.A. (as he then was). (Justice Fish subsequently became a member of the Supreme Court of Canada. He was part of the majority in *The Queen v. Mann.*)

The facts of the case indicated that the police had a reasonable basis for establishing a roadblock. While it is true that they did not know whether the suspected robbers had been hidden under the canvas in the cargo area of the truck, it was not unreasonable for them to have a suspicion in this regard. And, once they uncovered the canvas, there was clear evidence of a felony, namely, the cigarettes.

It is true that the police did not conduct the search in an effort to protect themselves. They had no reason to believe that their safety, or the safety of others, was in danger. But, as the majority said in *The Queen v. Mann,* a lawful detention may be for the purpose of "securing evidence of a crime."

Justice Fish stated:

> A search incident to detention is a valid exercise of police powers at common law only if the detention is itself lawful....
>
> The search must be for a valid purpose that is rationally connected to the purposes of the initial detention. It must also be reasonably necessary: (1) to secure non-conscriptive evidence of a crime; (2) to protect the police or any member of the public from imminent danger; or (3) to discover and secure anything that could endanger the police, the person detained or any member of the public, or facilitate escape.

There was an underlying assumption in the search: The police acted in good faith. That is, they had reasonable grounds for establishing the roadblock. The crime had only recently been committed. The offence was in the area near the roadblock. The description of the robbers and the escape vehicle, while general, was followed by the police.

DIFFERENCES BETWEEN THE CASES

What the police did in *The Queen v. Murray* was quite different from what was done in *The Queen v. Mann*. All members of the Supreme Court of Canada agreed on this point. In *The Queen v. Mann,* the police had no reason to look inside the defendant's pocket. They had felt the outside of his clothing, and they were satisfied that Mann carried no concealed weapon.

The only reason the searching officer gave for looking inside Mann's pocket, having felt the small object, was "curiosity." It was not because the police had reason to believe Mann had committed a drug offence.

"CONSCRIPTIVE" EVIDENCE

The type of evidence seized in *The Queen v. Mann* is called "non-conscriptive" evidence. It is to be contrasted to "conscriptive" evidence. Here is the reason for the difference: The Charter states that no person is required to be a witness against himself/herself.

Non-conscriptive evidence is not, as such, taken from the body of the person (as is the case with DNA). Rather, it is evidence that exists "independently," such as the crack cocaine found on Mann. Non-conscriptive evidence, if properly obtained, will not affect the fairness of a trial. That is, it will not affect the Charter right of the accused against self-incrimination.

Conscriptive evidence, however, occurs when an accused, in violation of that person's Charter rights, is compelled to incriminate himself/herself by means of a statement, the use of the body, or the production of bodily samples.

AN UNANSWERED 911 CALL: A RIGHT TO SEARCH?

In the *Queen v. Mann,* Justice Iacobucci spoke of the role of the Supreme Court of Canada in developing the common law as to permissible bounds for searches under the Charter. He said that in the absence of rules set down by Parliament, the Court would have to fashion principles out of individual cases where the facts might vary widely. What follows is an example of that fact variation.

The number used for an emergency call to the police for help is 911. It is recognized throughout Canada (and, indeed, throughout North America). Generally, there is a quick response to such calls.

A high priority for police response are 911 hang-ups. Without hesitation, police are sent to the caller's address. The assumption is that there may be a real, possibly life-threatening, emergency. The police who are dispatched do not know what to expect. It is the policy of many police departments, including those in Ontario, to send a patrol car with two officers who, in turn, are backed up by two other officers.

In Ontario, on June 1, 1992, police officers Clafton and Baldesarra were dispatched to the home of Vincent Godoy. Radio dispatch (911) had received a hang-up call. At about 1:30 a.m., the officers arrived at the Godoy home and knocked on the door. Godoy responded, partially opening the door. The officers asked if there was any "problem." Godoy answered that there was no problem. Officer Clafton asked if they could enter to check for themselves as to any problem. Godoy tried to shut the door, but was blocked from doing so. The officers forced entry. They did so though they neither heard nor saw anything which would have suggested that anyone was in distress.

Once inside the home, the officers heard a woman crying. They found Godoy's common law wife in the bedroom, curled in the fetal position and sobbing. She told the officers, who saw considerable swelling above her left eye, that Godoy had hit her. Godoy was placed under arrest. He struggled. Officer Baldesarra's finger was broken. Godoy was further charged with assaulting a police officer with the intent of resisting arrest. At trial, Godoy's wife testified that he had not struck her, but the charge of assaulting a police officer remained.

A central question was whether the officers had violated section 8 of the Charter by forcing their way into Godoy's home and searching it without a warrant.

THE SUPREME COURT OF CANADA DECIDES

The case was *The Queen v. Godoy*, [1999] 1 *Supreme Court Reports* 311, decided by a unanimous decision on the part of the nine members of the Court. It affirmed the right of the police to enter the Godoy home and search. Then Chief Justice Lamer wrote the opinion for the Court. He stated:

> The point of the 911 emergency response system is to provide whatever assistance is required under the circumstances of the call. In the context of a disconnected 911 call, the nature of the distress is unknown. However, in my view, it is reasonable, indeed imperative, that the police assume that the caller is in some distress and requires immediate assistance. To act otherwise would seriously impair the effectiveness of the system and undermine its very purpose.
>
> *The police duty to protect life is therefore engaged whenever it can be inferred that the 911 caller is or may be in some distress, including cases where the call is disconnected before the nature of the emergency can be determined* [emphasis added].

It is true that the Charter in section 8 provides a right to individual privacy, but the chief justice said that there really was no alternative available to the police but to force entry to the Godoy home. He said that suggestions that the police listen at the door, or check with neighbours as to any signs of distress, were impractical and possibly dangerous.

For the Court, the chief justice stated:

> Dignity, integrity and autonomy are the very values engaged in a most immediate and pressing nature by a disconnected 911 call. In such a case, the concern that a person's life or safety might be in danger is enhanced. Therefore, the interest of the person who seeks assistance by dialing 911 is closer to the core of the values of dignity, integrity and autonomy than the interest of the person who seeks to deny entry to police who arrive in response to the call for help.

THE U.S. EXPERIENCE WITH ROADBLOCKS

The constitutions of both the United States and Canada, as noted, prohibit unreasonable search and seizure. The U.S. approach to the subject in general, as we have said, has been cited and, to some extent, approved by the Supreme Court of Canada. What follows is a 6–3 decision of the U.S. Supreme Court in a 2000 case, *The City of Indianapolis v. Edmond,* November 28, 2000. Justice Sandra Day O'Connor wrote the majority decision, and Chief Justice William Rehnquist, joined by Justices Antonin Scalia and Clarence Thomas, dissented.

The city of Indianapolis established a police program of roadblocks primarily to catch drug offenders, but also for the purpose of checking drivers' licenses and vehicle registrations. This is how the program worked in 1998: Based on crime statistics and traffic flow within the city, Indianapolis police set up roadblocks, which often were planned weeks in advance. Generally, the stops were during daylight hours, and they were announced in advance by use of lighted signs: "Narcotics Checkpoint X-Miles Ahead, Narcotics K-9 in Use, Be Prepared to Stop."

About thirty police officers were stationed at each checkpoint. A set number of vehicles were pulled from the line of traffic. Under rules set by the city police chief, an officer was to approach each vehicle and tell the driver that this was a narcotics checkpoint, and that the stop would be brief. The driver was to be asked for his/her license and registration. The officer was to determine visually if there were signs of "impairment," and do "an open-view inspection from outside the vehicle." While this was done, another officer would walk a narcotics-sniffing dog around the vehicle.

A search was to be made — with the possibility of an arrest to follow — only if there were signs that the dog smelled narcotics, or if the officer's visual inspection resulted in specific suspicion of wrongdoing. (A search could also be made if the driver consented.) Typically, each stop was not to last more than five minutes. The police rules also emphasized that the vehicles stopped were not to be pulled out of sequence. Also, each search was to be made in the same way.

Six times between August and November 1998, the Indianapolis police set up roadblocks on city streets. A total of 1,161 cars were stopped at these roadblocks, and 104 motorists were arrested. Fifty-five of the arrests were drug-related, meaning that 5 percent of the total number of stops resulted in successful drug "hits." Forty-nine arrests were for conduct unrelated to drugs — such as driving with an expired driver's license — for an overall hit rate of 9 percent. (The average stop took about two to three minutes.)

THE U.S. SUPREME COURT DECIDES

In a 6–3 opinion, the U.S. Supreme Court struck down the Indianapolis roadblock program, as it was designed and used. The reason: The program was designed primarily as a general means for crime control. That was not a good enough reason to overcome the Fourth Amendment's requirement that police searches and seizures are generally unreasonable unless there is specific suspicion of wrongdoing. There are exceptions to this rule which would allow for "suspicionless" searches and seizures. But, those exceptions are driven, for the most part, by special needs beyond those of general law enforcement. Speaking for the Court majority, Justice O'Connor wrote:

> We have never approved a checkpoint program whose primary purpose was to detect evidence of ordinary criminal wrongdoing. Rather, our checkpoint cases have recognized only limited exceptions to the general rule that a seizure must be accompanied by some measure of individualized suspicion. We [have] suggested [in earlier cases] that we would not credit the "general interest in crime control" as justification for a regime of suspicionless stops. Consistent with this suggestion, each of the checkpoint programs that we have approved was designed primarily to serve purposes closely related to the problems of policing the border or the necessity of ensuring roadway safety. Because the primary purpose of the Indianapolis narcotics checkpoint program is to uncover evidence of ordinary criminal wrongdoing, the program contravenes the Fourth Amendment.

Still, shouldn't the Court have taken notice of the "severe and intractable" nature of the "drug problem" in the United States? Isn't the size of that problem sufficient reason for allowing brief roadblock checks? Justice O'Connor answered:

> Petitioners also emphasize the severe and intractable nature of the drug problem as justification for the checkpoint program. There is no doubt that traffic in illegal narcotics creates social harms of the first magnitude. The law enforcement problems that the drug trade creates likewise remain daunting and complex, particularly in light of the myriad forms of spin-off crime that it spawns. The same can be said of various other illegal activities, if only to a lesser degree. But the gravity of the threat alone cannot be dispositive of questions concerning what means law enforcement officers may employ to pursue a given purpose. Rather, *in determining whether individualized suspicion is required, we must consider the nature of the interests threatened and their connection to the particular law enforcement practices at issue. We are particularly reluctant to recognize exceptions to the general rule of individualized suspicion where governmental authorities primarily pursue their general crime control ends* [emphasis added].
>
> The primary purpose of the Indianapolis narcotics checkpoints is, in the end, to advance the general interest in crime control. We decline to suspend the usual requirement of individualized suspicion where the police seek to employ a checkpoint primarily for the ordinary enterprise of investigating crimes. We cannot sanction stops justified only by the generalized and ever-present

possibility that interrogation and inspection may reveal that any given motorist has committed some crime.

DISSENTING OPINION

Chief Justice Rehnquist, joined by Justices Scalia and Thomas, dissented. They argued, in large part, that highway roadblocks requiring regular brief stops are far different from the search of one's body or one's home. And, he stated, the applicable standards for passing upon whether a checkpoint seizure is lawful under the Fourth Amendment ought to be less stringent. The chief justice wrote:

> The lowered expectation of privacy in one's automobile is coupled with the limited nature of the intrusion: a brief, standardized, nonintrusive seizure. The brief seizure of an automobile can hardly be compared to the intrusive search of the body or the home. Thus, just as the "special needs" inquiry serves to both define and limit the permissible scope of those searches, the balancing test serves to define and limit the permissible scope of automobile seizures.
>
> Because of these extrinsic limitations upon roadblock seizures, the Court's new-found non-law-enforcement primary purpose test is both unnecessary to secure Fourth Amendment rights and bound to produce wide-ranging litigation over the purpose of any given seizure. Police designing highway roadblocks can never be sure of their validity, since a jury might later determine that a forbidden purpose exists. Roadblock stops may now be challenged on the grounds that they have some concealed forbidden purpose.

Efforts to enforce the law on public highways used by millions of motorists are obviously necessary to our society. The Court's opinion today casts a shadow over what had been assumed, on the basis of [other U.S. Supreme Court decisions], to be a perfectly lawful activity. Conversely, if the Indianapolis police had assigned a different purpose to their activity here, but in no way changed what was done on the ground to individual motorists, it might well be valid. The Court's non-law-enforcement primary purpose test simply does not serve as a proxy for anything that the Fourth Amendment is, or should be, concerned about in the automobile seizure context.

[The Indianapolis] program complies with our decisions regarding roadblock seizures of automobiles, and the addition of a dog sniff does not add to the length or the intrusion of the stop.

THE U.S. VIEW: DOES A "SNIFF" EQUAL A SEARCH?

In *City of Indianapolis v. Edmond,* the police used a narcotics-sniffing dog to walk around the stopped vehicle. Its job was to signal the officer if narcotics were likely to be found in the vehicle. The Court had to deal with the question as to whether the use of such a dog was a "search" within the meaning of the U.S. Constitution.

Justice O'Connor, speaking for the Court majority, referred to another decision in which she had written the majority opinion for the Court (6–3). The decision — *United States v. Place, 362 United States Supreme Court Reports* 696 (1983) — dealt with the use of canine sniffing dogs to inspect luggage for drugs, and she stated:

The Fourth Amendment protects people from unreasonable government intrusions into their legitimate expectations of privacy. We have affirmed that a person possesses a privacy interest in the contents of personal luggage that is protected by the Fourth Amendment....

A "canine sniff" by a well-trained narcotics detection dog, however, does not require opening the luggage. It does not expose non-contraband items that otherwise would remain hidden from public view, as does, for example, an officer's rummaging through the contents of the luggage. Thus, the manner in which information is obtained through this investigative technique is much less intrusive than a typical search.

Moreover, the sniff discloses only the presence or absence of narcotics, a contraband item. Thus, despite the fact that the sniff tells the authorities something about the contents of the luggage, the information obtained is limited. This limited disclosure also ensures that the owner of the property is not subjected to the embarrassment and inconvenience entailed in less discriminate and more intrusive investigative methods.

In these respects, the canine sniff is *sui generis* [in a class by itself]. We are aware of no other investigative procedure that is so limited both in the manner in which the information is obtained and in the content of the information revealed by the procedure. Therefore, we conclude that the particular course of investigation that the agents intended to pursue here — exposure of the respondent's luggage, which was located in a public place, to a trained canine

— did not constitute a "search" within the meaning of the Fourth Amendment.

USE OF "UNLAWFUL" EVIDENCE — *THE QUEEN V. MANN*

The drugs found on Mann and used to arrest and charge him were the result of an unlawful search within the meaning of the Charter. But, that, by itself, did not block the Crown from introducing them into evidence. This raised another question, and it brings us to the second part of the decision of the Supreme Court of Canada in *The Queen v. Mann.*

Here we find a division on the part of the Court. Justices Deschamps and Bastarache dissented from the majority opinion. They would have allowed the results of the unlawful search to be used in the trial of Mann. The majority refused to permit such use and, as a result, Mann was acquitted.

Both the majority and the dissenting opinions looked to the Charter to support their position. Both focused on section 24 of the Charter which provides:

> 24(1) Anyone whose rights or freedoms, as guaranteed by this Charter, have been infringed or denied may apply to a court of competent jurisdiction to obtain such remedy as the court considers appropriate and just in the circumstances.
>
> (2) Where, in proceedings under subsection (1), a court concludes that evidence was obtained in a manner that infringed or denied any rights or freedoms guaranteed by this Charter, the evidence shall be excluded if it is established that, having regard to all the circumstances, the admission of it in the proceedings would bring the administration of justice into disrepute.

Section 24(1) gives a court substantial discretion in fashioning a remedy for those whose Charter rights have been violated. However, it was to section 24(2) that both the majority and dissent turned to determine whether the drugs found from the unlawful search should be excluded from trial. The reason: section 24(2) is addressed to the specific problem of evidence exclusion from trial as a result of Charter violations.

THE MAJORITY OPINION

The majority set out three factors to be considered in finding whether evidence should be excluded under section 24(2):

1. the effect of admitting the evidence on the fairness of Mann's trial;
2. the seriousness of the questioned police conduct; and
3. the effects of excluding the evidence on the administration of justice.

Applying these factors, Justice Iacobucci, for the majority, stated:

> While a frisk search is a minimally intrusive search, the search of [Mann's] inner pocket must be weighed against the absence of any reasonable basis for justification. Individuals have a reasonable expectation of privacy in their pockets. The search here went beyond what was required to mitigate concerns about officer safety and reflects a serious breach of [Mann's] protection against unreasonable search and seizure.
>
> The final consideration is whether the exclusion of the evidence would adversely affect the administration of justice. In this case, there is little

doubt that the seized marijuana is the crux of the Crown's case against Mann. Exclusion of the evidence would substantially diminish, if not eliminate altogether, the Crown's case against [Mann].

Possession of marijuana for the purpose of trafficking remains a serious offence despite continuing debate about the extent of the harm associated with marijuana use. Regardless, *evidence which is non-conscriptive [such as bodily samples like hair] and essential to the Crown's case needs not necessarily be admitted* [emphasis added].

Just as there is no automatic exclusionary rule, there can be no automatic inclusion of the evidence either. The focus of the inquiry under this analysis is to balance the interests of truth with the integrity of the justice system. The nature of the fundamental rights at issue, and the lack of a reasonable foundation for the search, suggest that the inclusion of the evidence would adversely affect the administration of justice.

THE DISSENT

Justice Deschamps, joined by Justice Bastarache, as noted, dissented from the majority opinion. Essentially, while they agreed that the pat-down resulting in finding the drugs was the result of an unlawful search, they did not see this as a serious violation of the Charter. In the result, they would not have used section 24(2) to disqualify use of the evidence in Mann's drug trial. Justice Deschamps stated:

> I would like to clarify that it is not the intrusiveness of the search in the abstract which must be taken into consideration. Instead, what is to be

measured is the degree of intrusion relative to or over and above what would have been permissible under the circumstances.

This flows from the fact that what is being determined at this stage of the analysis is the seriousness of the Charter violation, not the seriousness of the search *per se*. If it was lawful in the present case for the officers to conduct a pat-down search, I find it difficult to see how taking the small additional step of unthinkingly giving in to curiosity, and slipping a hand into [Mann's] kangaroo pouch, can be regarded as sufficient to put the violation which occurred in the present case on the "serious" end of the spectrum. The legal part of the search which involved the touching of the body was much more intrusive than the illegal part, which saw the search extended into [Mann's] open pocket.

Turning to the amount of privacy [Mann] was reasonably entitled to expect at the time the incident in question occurred, I find it necessary to have regard to the fact that the search occurred late at night (approximately midnight) and in a "high-crime area," approximately two blocks from the scene of a break-in. Individuals should expect a lesser amount of privacy in public areas frequently patrolled by police than they do in their homes or offices, for example.

Finally, while the situation may not have been "urgent," and while the officers might not have had "reasonable and probable grounds," the application of all of the other criteria set out above does not, in my view, point to the conclusion that the violation which occurred in the present case was very serious.

[Further,] I disagree with the majority's conclusion that the inclusion of the evidence in the present case would adversely affect the administration of justice. With respect, I believe it is exclusion which would lead to this result.... The third stage of section 24(2) analysis turns essentially on the importance for the evidence to the case for the Crown and the gravity of the offence.

As Iacobucci J. points out, there is "little doubt that the seized marijuana is the crux of the Crown's case against [Mann]." The marijuana and "baggies" seized by the officers in the present case constitute the Crown's only evidence to the effect that the accused possessed the drug and intended to sell it at some point in the near future. In addition, the jurisprudence of this Court strongly supports the view that possession of marijuana for the purposes of trafficking (as opposed to mere possession) is a "serious" offence for the purposes of s. 24(2) of the Charter....

These factors favour admitting the evidence.

THE GOOD FAITH OF THE OFFICERS

Is the "good faith" of the police officers in making a pat-down resulting in an unlawful search a factor in deciding whether evidence should be excluded under section 24(2) of the Charter?

Yes, but there are limits. One such limit was applied by the majority in *The Queen v. Mann*. The majority ruled that "good faith cannot be claimed if a Charter violation is committed on the basis of a police officer's unreasonable error or ignorance as to the source of his or her authority." Moreover, the majority opinion stated that good faith alone will not meet the tests of section 24(2). Rather, it is "but one factor in the analysis and must be considered alongside other factors which speak to the seriousness of the breach."

Justice Deschamps, dissenting, stated: "The officer who conducted the search in the present case did not act in bad faith. There is no evidence that he knew he was acting outside the scope of his powers. Nor is it fair to characterise his error, as the majority does, as unreasonable. Mere 'curiosity' does not necessarily amount to bad faith."

REFERENCES AND FURTHER READING

* Cited by the Supreme Court of Canada.

Coughlan, Steve. "Search Based on Articulable Cause: Proceed with Caution or Full Stop?" *Criminal Reports* 6th ed. 2 (2002): 49.*

Greenhouse, Linda. "Supreme Court Bars Traffic Stops That are Intended as Drug Checks." *New York Times,* November 29, 2000.

Makin, Kirk. "Right to Privacy Diminished in Emergency, Court Rules." *Globe and Mail,* February 5, 1999.

Smith, Graeme. "Supreme Court Limits Police Frisking Rights." *Globe and Mail,* July 24, 2004.

Sopinka, John, Sidney N. Lederman, and Alan W. Bryant. *The Law of Evidence in Canada*, 2nd ed. Toronto: Butterworths, 1999.*

Stribopoulos, James. "A Failed Experiment? Investigative Detention: Ten Years Later." *Alberta Law Review* 41 (2003): 335.*

Young, Alan. "All Along the Watchtower: Arbitrary Detention and the Police Function." *Osgoode Hall Law Journal 329* (1991): 29.*

CHAPTER 4

HYPNOSIS: AN AID IN CSI?

In a criminal investigation, police are concerned with finding the facts: Was there a crime? And, if there was a crime, who was the wrongdoer? The investigatory trail is not taken in terms of any presumption of innocence — only the facts that brought the police to the scene. This is not to say that the police are not concerned with how a court would look at the elements of a case should the Crown lay charges. Here fairness of investigation, partly defined by the Charter, certainly comes into play. This chapter is a blending of the law as it impacts on police investigation techniques and the results flowing from those techniques at trial.

Our subject matter is the role of science in finding facts and, later, the use of science in the proof of alleged facts at trial. We will find that calling something "science" does not, in itself, make the facts found clear beyond a reasonable doubt. Nor do the conclusions drawn by someone who professes himself/herself an "expert" necessarily qualify that person's findings as irreversible.

Among the subjects we will discuss are hypnosis and pathology. They are subjects that at times might help crime scene investigators and the Crown in laying and proving criminal charges — but that in their implementation may hinder investigation and, in the final analysis, the administration of justice. We begin with hypnosis and its use in a criminal murder trial.

The principal case discussed is *The Queen v. Stephen John Trochym*, [2007] 1 Supreme *Court of Canada Reports* 239. It is a murder case in which Stephen John Trochym was charged with the second degree murder of his girlfriend. This is how Justice Deschamps, who wrote the majority decision for the Court, began her opinion:

> In recent years, a number of public inquiries have highlighted the importance of safeguarding the criminal justice system — and protecting the accused who are tried under it — from the possibility of wrongful conviction. As this Court has previously noted: "The names of Marshall, Milgaard, Morin, Sophonow and Parsons signal prudence and caution in a murder case." *United States v. Burns*, [2001] 1 *Supreme Court of Canada Reports* 283 [these were cases in which real questions were raised as to the alleged guilt of those convicted]....
> In this [case], we consider once again the need to carefully scrutinize evidence presented against an accused for reliability and prejudicial effect, and to ensure the basic fairness of the criminal process.

We will set out the facts relating to the homicide. Our starting-point in this introduction, however, is to note that the subject of the Supreme Court's inquiry went to the right of the Crown to use hypnosis evidence as an important piece of the Crown's case against Trochym — helping a neighbour of the victim recall through hypnosis whether she saw Trochym leaving the victim's apartment on a Wednesday or a Thursday. Placing Trochym at the crime scene on Wednesday at the time recalled by the neighbour would significantly assist the Crown's case because it would come within the time the murder was committed.

First, we will describe the intersect between memory and hypnosis. Then, we will outline how hypnosis evidence had been used in criminal trials for more than thirty years — up to the time of the Trochym decision. It was in the lower courts, not the Supreme Court of Canada, where guidelines were set for the use of evidence resulting from hypnotism. As a result of the Trochym decision, this practice was changed.

Among the questions raised in this chapter are:

- Is memory recall through hypnotism likely to be accurate?
- When and under what conditions may a "new" or "novel" science be challenged in a criminal court?
- May defence counsel agree to allow otherwise improper hypnotism evidence to be presented to the jury?
- Even if hypnotism evidence has been improperly received, is it possible for a jury verdict of guilty to still be upheld?

HYPNOSIS: BACKGROUND

Hypnosis is an induced mental state. It focuses the mind in a narrow area and, at the same time, it bypasses or distracts the conscious mind. The hypnotic state is not the same as natural physical sleep. Parts of the brain are active in hypnosis in the same way as during one's waking hours. But, in hypnosis the mind becomes relaxed. The body also may become relaxed. However, that is only a means to induce the hypnotic state.

Once under hypnosis, the mind becomes receptive to facts, ideas, and concepts that usually are not significantly at variance from personal beliefs, values, attitudes, and desires.

A hypnotic state is characterized by *trance*. There are four trances. The first stage, a *light trance*, is one familiar to most as "natural." It is like daydreaming. The activities around the individual tend to be turned off until the daydream is interrupted. For example, to induce a subject to become involved in weight control, only the light trance generally is needed.

The *medium trance* occurs when the subject's breathing changes. There tends to be a shorter breathing rhythm. Relaxation becomes deeper. The head often rolls forward. Muscle tone diminishes. Imagination becomes stronger. Feel, smell, and taste created in the mind can be imagined.

Then, there is a *deep trance*. The subject can feel detached and sense lightness, even floating. The hypnotist's voice may appear to fade in and out. And, through suggestion, the subject may have greater muscle tone.

The final stage is *very deep hypnosis*. Here, the subject is aware of his/her surroundings and can hear conversations and requests. A verbal response, however, seems to be too much of an effort. At this stage, there can be a sense of euphoria.

HOW MEMORY WORKS

Our focus is the relationship between hypnosis and memory. Specifically, we will look at whether the law allows hypnosis to be used for memory recall. Here, it must be emphasized, we are dealing with judge-made law. In the Trochym decision, the Supreme Court of Canada looked to its own rulings and other judicial decisions to determine the lines to be drawn in the use of hypnosis to refresh memory.

However, Justice Deschamps, who wrote the majority decision in *Trochym*, made it clear that those rulings were rooted in science — and science is an evolving subject. That which may appear to be true today might be disproved in the future. And the courts must be prepared to deal with new factual realities.

Of hypnosis and memory, Justice Deschamps stated:

While hypnosis may assist witnesses to recall additional detail, the medical community knows very little about how memory functions or what role hypnosis may have in recalling and/or altering memories.

The general consensus appears to be that memory does not work like a tape recorder that can be played back but, rather, is constructive or additive. Remembering may therefore be a more creative mental process than it is usually understood to be. Given these gaps in scientific knowledge, the admission of post-hypnosis memories raises a number of concerns.

The Crown's expert, Dr. Matheson, testified that "the general understanding is that, if properly and professionally done, you would probably get more information [through hypnosis], and that information will be a combination of accurate and inaccurate [information]."

Justice Deschamps described three factors that can account for the high rate of real memory error flowing from hypnotism recall. She stated:

The first, and most significant, of these is the risk of confabulation, or the creation of hallucinated or false memories. Confabulation can result from the power of express or implied suggestions, or simply from a strong, unconscious desire to compensate for a lack of actual memory. It may also result from other causes that are unknown, because scientists know very little about memory. All three expert witnesses in *Trochym* noted at trial that, while confabulation may also occur without hypnosis, a person's suggestibility is enhanced under hypnosis.

A second, and related, factor is that a person's critical faculty appears to be reduced while he or she is under hypnosis. As Dr. Pollock, one of two expert witnesses called by the defence, explained, a person who has a memory in the normal "waking state" will examine it and decide whether it is accurate and should be reported. A hypnotized person is more likely to report whatever comes to his or her mind. As a result, *while hypnosis may help a witness recall an event in greater detail, this heightened recollection may simply contain both more correct and more false details. The greater number of details the witness remembers may therefore create the illusion that his or her memory has improved in accuracy* [emphasis added].

Finally, experts express concern about the potential for "memory hardening," a process by which a person who has been hypnotized becomes increasingly, and unduly, confident in his or her memories. The exact cause of memory hardening is unknown but the phenomenon has been recognized. It is described as the "most consistent finding of all in studies on the various effects of hypnosis." This process is undetectable and seemingly irreversible. When combined with the possibility that memories have been tainted through confabulation, improperly phrased questions, or other unintentional influences, the danger that the accused will be denied a fair hearing becomes obvious.

CONFABULATION DEFINED

Suggestion, through hypnosis, can result in *false memory*. That is, the individual does not remember, for example, a particular incident. In hypnosis, however, the subject is given a suggestion as to the forgotten event. The suggestion can become part of the memory. Imagination fills a gap not recalled by memory. That is, the suggestion provided in hypnotism becomes reality. This is called *confabulation*.

CHALLENGE QUESTION

IS EYEWITNESS EVIDENCE INFALLIBLE?

Q. Aren't the dangers of post-hypnotic evidence noted by Justice Deschamps also to be found in so-called "eyewitness" evidence? Suppose Sam witnessed a robbery. He saw the robber. Police ask Sam for eyewitness identification. Are there possibilities of confabulation and memory hardening that might taint Sam's testimony?

An expert witness in *Trochym* made this argument. His point seemed to be that the validity of such evidence is best determined by the trial judge and through the process of examination and cross-examination. This, said the expert, allows for a meaningful context to be set for weighing the credibility of the witness' eyewitness evidence.

Justice Deschamps, for the majority in *Trochym*, rejected the argument. She stated:

> Hypnosis introduces more sources of
> concern and a likelihood that existing

fragilities of human memory will increase, tainting the reliability of the evidence. Furthermore, the frailties of human memory when unaffected by hypnosis are only just starting to become known; indeed, the fallibility of eyewitness identification has been a central concern in a number of inquiries into wrongful convictions.

In his public inquiry into the wrongful conviction of Thomas Sophonow, for example, the Honourable Peter deC. Cory observed that most triers of fact have implicit faith in eyewitness identification and that this can be hazardous. He recommended, among other things, instructing the jury about the shortcomings of eyewitness identification and cautioning that the vast majority of wrongful convictions have resulted from faulty eyewitness identification: *The Inquiry Regarding Thomas Sophonow: The Investigation, Prosecution and Consideration of Entitlement to Compensation* (2001), at pp. 33–34. While Justice Cory was specifically addressing ordinary memory, his recommendations make it all the more clear why a technique used to enhance memory must be approached with great caution.

POST-HYPNOTIC EVIDENCE: PAST DECISIONS

The Trochym case testing the validity of post-hypnotic evidence was the first to reach the Supreme Court of Canada. But the legal question had been addressed by lower Canadian courts for some time. And, as Justice Deschamps stated in the Trochym decision, the lower courts had reached a common approach following rather specific guidelines laid out in 1984 by the Alberta Court of Queen's Bench in *The Queen v. Clark,* 13 *Canadian Criminal Cases* (3d series) 117. These were the guidelines:

- The person conducting the hypnotic interview should be a qualified professional.
- The hypnotist must be independent of the party who requires her/his services.
- The hypnotist should be given only the minimum amount of information necessary to conduct the interview.
- The entire interview between the hypnotist and the potential witness should be recorded, preferably on videotape.
- The interview should be conducted with only the hypnotist and the subject present.
- Prior to the actual hypnosis of the subject, the hypnotist should conduct a lengthy interview of the subject to determine his medical history, including information about the present or past use of drugs.
- Prior to hypnosis, the hypnotist should elicit from the subject a detailed description of the facts surrounding the subject matter of the hypnosis session, as the subject is able to recall them at that point in time.
- The hypnotist should pay careful attention to the form and manner of his questions, the choice of his words, and the avoidance of body language, so that he is not either intentionally or inadvertently providing the subject with information.

Yet, bear in mind that the guidelines could be viewed as a filtering process through which proposed post-hypnosis evidence has to pass before it could even be considered by the finders of fact, whether jury or judge.

The party seeking to use such evidence must meet the conditions set out in the guidelines. This proof comes not in the trial itself. Rather, it comes in a kind of preliminary hearing called a *voir dire*. There, without the jury being present, the party seeking to use hypnosis evidence has to prove to a judge that the guidelines have been met. And, that is only the start in the proof of the weight they are to be given in a trial on the merits.

This does not mean that such evidence has to be accepted as fact. Rather, for example, if there were a jury trial, the judge and counsel are free to comment on limits to evidence derived through hypnosis. And, this means that the jury (or judge, if the matter were tried by a judge alone) could give such evidence limited weight.

(As we shall see, however, sometimes counsel believe that a jury might give evidence of hypnotism added weight because they believe that the results of hypnotism must be true. See, "Challenge Questions: Agreement Between Counsel.")

THE BASIS FOR THE DECISION IN *THE QUEEN V. CLARK*
In the Clark case, the accused was charged with two counts of first degree murder. He had no memory of the events until he was hypnotized. While there was no dispute that the accused had committed the acts with which he was charged, the issue at trial was his intent and mental capacity at the relevant time. In law, without the intent and lacking the mental capacity, he could not be convicted of the murder charges.

The trial judge in *Clark* noted concerns about the use of hypnosis, but concluded that it would only be in an "extraordinary case" that a court would deny a witness from testifying after having his or her memory stimulated by hypnosis. However, he held that "the content of the hypnosis session is a proper subject for inquiry at the trial because it bears heavily on the credibility of the witness and the weight to be given his evidence."

To this end, the trial judge set out a number of principles that should guide a hypnotist during a hypnosis session. He observed that these guidelines (as listed above) would improve the reliability of evidence obtained under hypnosis. Again, it should be emphasized that the results of hypnosis, if allowed, in the past have been used by both the Crown and the defence.

REJECTING THE "CLARK APPROACH"

In the Trochym decision, Justice Deschamps acknowledged that the *Clark* guidelines had been used by lower courts for a number of years. But she said that the basic science was lacking to support those guidelines. In no small measure, the reason for rejecting what the lower courts had followed came from the expert, himself, who initially gave the rationale and support to cause those guidelines to be adopted.

Justice Deschamps wrote:

> It should be noted that *Hurd* (*State v. Hurd,* 414 *Atlantic Reports* 2d series 291 (New Jersey Supreme Court) 1980), which formed the basis for the *Clark* guidelines, has come to be revisited, in part as a result of the views expressed since then by Dr. Martin Orne, whose expert testimony had played a central role in that case.
>
> Dr. Orne subsequently warned that "hypnotically induced memories should never be permitted to form the basis for testimony by witnesses or victims in a court of law" *Burral v. State,* 724 Atlantic Reports 2d series 65 (Maryland Supreme Court 1999), at p. 81. He was of the view that "there is a considerable risk that the inherent unreliability of information confidently provided by a hypnotized person may actually be detrimental to the

truth-seeking process" (*State v. Moore*, 902 Atlantic Reports 2d series 1212 (New Jersey Supreme Court 2006) at p. 1228). *After reconsidering the inherent unreliability of post-hypnosis testimony, New Jersey joined the 26 states in the United States that limit the admissibility of post-hypnosis testimony. In New Jersey, post-hypnosis testimony is now generally inadmissible in a criminal trial* [emphasis added].

Since the *Clark* guidelines are derived from Dr. Orne's testimony in *Hurd*, it would be disturbing for this Court to blind itself to the subsequent developments in the American cases. With the basic reliability of post-hypnosis evidence increasingly in question, judicial approaches to such evidence have tended to shift from an assessment of the weight to be attributed to post-hypnosis testimony to whether it should even be admissible.

THE FACTS IN *THE QUEEN V. TROCHYM*

The majority opinion in *Trochym* only gave sparse treatment to the underlying facts. The primary focus of the opinion centred on the broad question of the use of post-hypnotic evidence in a criminal trial. However, the dissent in *Trochym* treated the facts in substantial detail. This is what Justice Bastarache, for the dissent, wrote:

Ms. Haghnegahdar [the woman who claimed to be a witness] was first interviewed by Constable Pike on October 17, 1992, the day following the discovery of Ms. Hunter's body. She told him, among other things, that she had seen Mr. Trochym come out of Ms. Hunter's apartment on Thursday, October 15, 1992, at 3:00 p.m. as she was getting home from school. At this time, the police were conducting routine interviews of all Ms. Hunter's neighbours to determine whether any of them had any relevant information that would assist the investigation.

The next afternoon, Detectives Clarke and McCulla did a follow-up interview with Ms. Haghnegahdar. The meeting was audio-taped and heard at the *voir dire*. During the meeting, she expressed confusion over whether she saw the appellant leaving the apartment on Wednesday or Thursday. At this early point in the investigation, the police had not conclusively placed the time of death in the early morning hours of Wednesday, October 14, as most of the evidence that led to this conclusion had yet to be investigated. Nor did they know there were other witnesses placing Mr. Trochym at the apartment building on the afternoon of Wednesday, October 14. Mr. Raymer, the building superintendent, and his babysitter, Ms. Humenick, gave statements to seeing Mr. Trochym on the Wednesday only after this second interview with Ms. Haghnegahdar.

Only after receiving these statements from Mr. Raymer and Ms. Humenick did the police contemplate Ms. Haghnegahdar undergoing hypnosis in order to clear up the day of the sighting. The session was arranged for November 8, to be carried out by Dr. Matheson. In arranging the session, police made sure to convey as little information as possible about the investigation to either Dr. Matheson or Ms. Haghnegahdar, so to avoid any potential influence leading up to the session.

On the day of the session, Ms. Haghnegahdar was driven to Dr. Matheson's office by Detective McCulla. The officer testified to being careful not to impart any information concerning the case or making suggestions regarding the information sought from her during their contact. At Dr. Matheson's office, Ms. Haghnegahdar and Dr. Matheson were introduced in the waiting room and then Detective McCulla and Dr. Matheson met privately so that he could be given a brief overview of the case. This conversation was videotaped and heard at the *voir dire*. Detective McCulla gave Dr. Matheson the basic facts of the case and told him that Ms. Haghnegahdar saw Mr. Trochym leaving the apartment and was confused in her second interview about whether she saw him on Wednesday or Thursday. Detective McCulla told the doctor that the police would like to have the day and time of the sighting cleared up, but did not indicate or suggest to Dr. Matheson which day they would prefer the sighting to have been.

Next, Detective McCulla left and the session between Dr. Matheson and Ms. Haghnegahdar began. The entire hypnosis session between Dr. Matheson and Ms. Haghnegahdar was videotaped and heard at the *voir dire*. The hypnosis consisted of Dr. Matheson putting Ms. Haghnegahdar into a very relaxed state. Once in this state, he asked her to describe the event of seeing Mr. Trochym coming out of Ms. Hunter's apartment on her way home from school. At this point, she recalled more details than before, such as the colour of his clothing being "dark" and a "scary" look he gave her.

After describing this, Dr. Matheson asked her to describe what happened afterwards, specifically what she did once she arrived at her own apartment and for the rest of the day. Through this she recalled that she had a snack, then took a nap, was woken up by her alarm clock and had wanted to go back to sleep but did not because she was worried she would be late to pick up her daughter who was at piano class until 5:00 p.m. She then described going to pick up her daughter. At one point, Dr. Matheson asked: "Just notice what day is it?", to which Ms. Haghnegahdar responded: "Oh every Wednesday, every Wednesday she has to practice, piano practice...." It was by associating having to pick up her daughter from piano lessons, which were always on Wednesdays, with seeing Mr. Trochym coming out of the apartment that same day, that Ms. Haghnegahdar was able to determine that she saw him on Wednesday as opposed to Thursday.

In the post-hypnosis interview with Detective McCulla immediately following the session, Ms. Haghnegahdar confirmed that her memory of seeing Mr. Trochym on Wednesday was directly associated with having to pick up her daughter from her piano lesson that day. As well, Ms. Haghnegahdar reiterated those details she recalled in the session concerning his attire when she saw him. "We — I — I saw him ah with the dark a dark jacket and dark pants and before I didn't remember but after I had been hypnotized I remember his jacket was ah zipped up to under his ah cheek," as well as his "scary eyes." I note that she did not say during this interview that Mr. Trochym was wearing a leather coat or windbreaker. The interview between

Detective McCulla and Ms. Haghnegahdar was videotaped and heard at the *voir dire* [the special hearing on the post-hypnotic evidence itself].

There was one more interview between the police and Ms. Haghnegahdar that took place on November 10, 1992. The sole purpose of this interview was to show her a picture of the appellant to see if this was the same man she claimed to have seen leaving Ms. Hunter's around 3:00 p.m. on Wednesday, October 14.

During the *voir dire*, the trial judge heard five days' worth of evidence. The Crown called Detectives McCulla and Clarke and Dr. Matheson to testify to their interaction with Ms. Haghnegahdar and each other. The defence called two expert witnesses, Dr. Pollock, a clinical psychologist, working in the therapeutic application of hypnosis, and Dr. Yarmey, an expert on memory.

The defence experts were able to raise a couple of concerns about adherence to the *Clark* guidelines (*R. v. Clark* (1984), 13 *C.C.C.* (3d) 117 (Alta. Q.B.)), though these were fairly trivial. First, Dr. Pollock noted that the information concerning the case given to Dr. Matheson was not in writing as required by guideline 3, but instead was oral and was videotaped. However, he admitted on cross-examination that they still fulfilled the purpose intended by the guidelines, that is, to monitor and minimize the risk of inadvertently conveying information to the hypnotist. Second, both Dr. Pollock and Dr. Yarmey suggested that Dr. Matheson may have unintentionally assumed that Ms. Haghnegahdar was recovering memory by linking events together when it was possible that she was not, and this may have influenced her. The trial judge found, however, in the context of the session as a whole that Dr. Matheson's assumption did not seem unreasonable or suggestive....

Dr. Pollock also talked about confabulation and the difficulty, even for the hypnotist, of determining which refreshed memories might be real and which might be imagined. The potential for a subject to be overly confident in their new memories and for "memory hardening" to occur were also identified. As well, both Dr. Pollock and Dr. Yarmey raised concerns about the possibility of pre- and post-hypnosis suggestion. On cross-examination, the Crown was able to demonstrate that none of these concerns were live concerns with regards to Ms. Haghnegahdar's evidence. Both defence experts conceded that independent corroboration of hypnotically refreshed memories was one way to assess its reliability. Dr. Pollock also clarified this for the trial judge:

THE COURT: And one of the mechanisms whereby a recovered memory can be evaluated is by making that memory referable to other known facts?

WITNESS: Yes, that's true. If there is external, independent corroboration of the recollection.

THE COURT: So one should approach memories that have been "recovered" through hypnosis with some measure of scepticism, and one should look for other evidence capable of confirming the reliability of those recovered memories?

WITNESS: Yes, very definitely.

CHALLENGE QUESTIONS

AGREEMENT BETWEEN COUNSEL

The trial judge in *Trochym* allowed this agreement between the Crown and defence counsel: The Crown was permitted to introduce post-hypnotic evidence of Gity Haghnegahdar, the neighbour of the murdered woman. That evidence went to the day and time when the neighbour saw the accused, Trochym, leaving the victim's apartment.

The agreement between counsel called on the Crown not to make any mention of the fact that the evidence came as a result of hypnosis. In so doing, the Crown was allowed to say in closing argument to the jury that the neighbour's evidence was uncontested.

Q. Why would defence counsel have entered such an agreement that, on its face, would seem to be hurtful to his client? Was it "improper" for the trial judge to have allowed the agreement?

The agreement brought comment from the majority and the dissent in *Trochym*. Justice Deschamps, for the majority, made it clear that their view was that the agreement was inappropriate. She stated:

> As a result of the agreement entered into by the parties, defence counsel did not cross-examine Ms. Haghnegahdar about her pre-hypnosis statements and the jury was not informed that the witness had undergone hypnosis.

I do not doubt that this agreement came about because defence counsel wished to minimize the risk that the jury would give undue weight to the witness's testimony if it was informed that she had undergone hypnosis. However, the fact remains that the jury was left without the proper evidentiary basis on which to assess the accuracy of the witness' testimony. The prejudice caused by the absence of cross-examination was exacerbated by Crown counsel's closing remarks:

> Gity Haghnegahdar also testified that she saw the accused that same afternoon. Gity was certain that it was Wednesday, October 14, 1992, not some other Wednesday, and she was one hundred percent sure that it was the accused. [Defence counsel] was unable to shake her on that in cross-examination. She knew what week it was, she knew what day it was, she knew what time it was....
>
> Gity was sure of her evidence on these issues, and let's not forget she was interviewed that very week by the police, so the events were still fresh in her mind. It is not a case of someone who is interviewed months afterwards and asked to try to recall events. She [was] interviewed that very week.
>
> Since Crown counsel knew both that Ms. Haghnegahdar had in fact changed her statement regarding the day she saw the appellant and that defence

counsel was effectively prevented from cross-examining Ms. Haghnegahdar on the inconsistency between her pre- and post-hypnosis memories, it was unseemly for Crown counsel to characterize Ms. Haghnegahdar's testimony as being unshaken.

DISSENT

Justice Bastarache, for the three dissenting justices, stated:

I cannot agree that it was inappropriate for the trial judge to permit this agreement. It is argued that the impetus for the agreement between the defence and the Crown not to put the issue of Ms. Haghnegahdar's hypnosis before the jury was a concern by defence counsel that members of the jury might view hypnotically enhanced memories as infallible. As framed, this suggests that defence counsel's concern was that the jury would have heard that Ms. Haghnegahdar's memories had been refreshed by hypnosis and would have automatically and uncritically accepted these as true.

As I read the record of the discussions between defence and Crown counsel and the trial judge on this issue, there were two concerns motivating the defence to strike this deal, and these were strictly tactical and not born out of some fear that the jury would uncritically accept the hypnosis evidence.

The first appears to have been about the time it would take to put such evidence before the jury. Second, and relatedly, was a realization that the hypnosis evidence was quite credible and, if the jury were told that it was hypnosis evidence, they would be even more likely to believe Ms. Haghnegahdar....

I am of the view that juries should be informed of efforts to enhance memory, as they are quite capable of assessing this evidence and giving it proper weight. However, there is no absolute rule on this point, and agreements between counsel should be respected where no prejudice is shown to have been caused to a party.

Note: There was no discussion concerning the views of the investigating police officers.

YOU BE THE JUDGE

A CASE FOR THE CURATIVE PROVISION

The case that follows is real. It was raised in *The Queen* v. *Trochym.*

THE FACTS

The Supreme Court of Canada found that the post-hypnosis evidence in *Trochym* should not have been allowed. It should not have been presented to the jury. Still, the Crown argued that the error was not substantial enough to have affected the jury verdict of "guilty." It was a verdict that the trial court allowed.

THE ISSUE

Can a verdict of guilty be permitted even though a legal error occurred during the trial?

POINTS TO CONSIDER

- Even though a trial court made a legal error, a guilty verdict may be allowed if there has been no substantial wrong or miscarriage of justice. This result follows because of section 686(1)(b)(iii) of the Criminal Code which states:

  On the hearing of an appeal against a conviction or against a verdict that the appellant is unfit to stand trial or not criminally responsible on account of mental disorder, the court of appeal (a) may allow the appeal where it is of the opinion that (ii) the judgment of the trial court should be set aside on the ground of a wrong decision on a question of law, or (b) may dismiss the appeal where (iii) notwithstanding that the court is of the opinion that on any ground mentioned in subparagraph (a)(ii) the appeal might be decided in favour of the appellant, *it is of the opinion that no substantial wrong or miscarriage of justice has occurred* [emphasis added].

- One class of errors to which section 686 applies is called "harmless errors." These are errors of a minor nature that can have no practical impact on the verdict.
- A second class of errors under section 686 includes "serious" errors which would justify a new trial but for the fact that the evidence presented at trial was so overwhelming that a reviewing court concludes there was no substantial wrong or miscarriage of justice.
- The Trochym case was a jury trial. It is the function of the jury to determine the facts and return a verdict. As such, the jury makes no findings of fact. Its deliberations are conducted in secret.

DISCUSSION

In *Trochym,* Justice Deschamps refused to allow the guilty verdict to stand under section 686(1)(b)(iii) of the Criminal Code. She ruled that the error on the part of the trial court judge in allowing post-hypnotic evidence was serious.

Whether there was no substantial wrong or miscarriage of justice, she said, was a matter to be determined under a high standard. It is not enough to base it on that required in proving a case against a defendant in a criminal trial: proof beyond a reasonable doubt. More is required under section 686(1)(b)(iii) because the appellate court was not present at trial. The evidence must be so overwhelming that the reviewing court would conclude there was no substantial wrong or miscarriage of justice. There was no way, as such, for the appellate judge to measure what went through the minds of the jurors.

Justice Deschamps wrote:

> This standard should not be equated with the ordinary standard in a criminal trial of proof beyond a reasonable doubt. The application of the proviso to serious errors reflects a higher standard appropriate to appellate review. The standard applied by an appellate court, namely that the evidence against an accused is so overwhelming that conviction is inevitable or would invariably result, is a substantially higher one than the requirement that the Crown prove its case "beyond a reasonable doubt" at trial.
>
> This higher standard reflects the fact that it is difficult for an appellate court, in particular when considering a jury trial, since no detailed findings of fact will have

been made, to consider retroactively the effect that, for example, excluding certain evidence could reasonably have had on the outcome.

This is not a case where I can conclude that there is no reasonable possibility that the verdict would have been different had the errors not been made. The post-hypnosis evidence, considered critical by the Crown and characterized as significant by the judge, has to be excluded.... Once [this] evidence is withdrawn, it cannot be said that the remaining evidence "is so overwhelming that [the] trier of fact would inevitably convict."

THE DISSENT

Justice Bastarache, for the dissent, detailed the facts of the case as they were presented to the jury. In doing so, he noted that the trial itself took fourteen weeks. He recalled that the Crown brought forward more than forty witnesses.

The testimony of the Crown witnesses, said Justice Bastarache, in part went to the increasingly difficult relationship between Trochym and the victim. On the whole, it can be said that the evidence portrayed Trochym as a controlling and jealous person.

The evidence, again from several witnesses, made it clear that the victim, both before and close to the time of her murder, had told friends that she intended to end her relationship with Trochym.

Justice Bastarache stated:

> But more importantly, I do not think that there is any reasonable possibility that the verdict would have been different without the error.... I would add that I would disagree with the assertion by Deschamps J. ... that the standard required for application of the curative proviso is higher than that required for a conviction, and I know of no authority supporting that proposition. [The curative proviso or provision allows a court to substitute a judgment if no substantial wrong or miscarriage of justice would result.]
>
> Indeed, in my view, the evidence against Mr. Trochym was so overwhelming that I have no hesitation applying the curative provisions of §686(1)(b)(iii).
>
> Even excluding the hypnotically enhanced memories of Ms. Haghnegahdar of seeing the appellant leaving [the victim's] apartment on Wednesday, as my colleague proposes to do, leaves us with her initial evidence of seeing him on Thursday — a time when her murdered body was inside the apartment.
>
> Furthermore, Mr. Trochym had motive and the opportunity to murder [the victim], and a stranger would not have returned to rearrange the crime scene and move the body. He also seems to have

known the means of her death before an innocent party could. Moreover, Mr. Trochym's version of events on key issues was contradicted by more than half of the more than forty Crown witnesses who testified. Even excluding all of the impugned evidence, as my colleague would, we are still left with a great deal of highly probative [acceptable in law] evidence in support of the Crown's case.

THE ROLE OF THE CROWN AND THE ROLE OF THE COURTS AS SEEN BY THE MAJORITY AND THE DISSENT IN *THE QUEEN V. TROCHYM*

THE MAJORITY (JUSTICE DESCHAMPS)

It cannot be over-emphasized that the purpose of a criminal prosecution is not to obtain a conviction; it is to lay before a jury what the Crown considers to be credible evidence relevant to what is alleged to be a crime. Counsel have a duty to see that all available legal proof of the facts is presented; it should be done firmly and pressed to its legitimate strength but it must also be done fairly. The role of prosecutor excludes any notion of winning or losing; his function is a matter of public duty ... and in civil life there can be none charged with greater personal responsibility. It is to be efficiently performed with an ingrained sense of the dignity, the seriousness and the justness of judicial proceedings.

THE DISSENT (JUSTICE BASTARACHE)

A general principle of criminal evidence law is that a just result in criminal trials is best achieved when the decision maker has all relevant and probative information before him or her.... When weighing probative value against prejudicial effect, this must be kept in mind. It must be recalled that prejudicial effect is the likelihood that the jury, even if properly instructed, will use the evidence for an improper purpose; it is not created merely by evidence that is unfavourable to a party's case.

Second, it must be recalled that our criminal justice system is an adversarial one. It is parties, not the trial judge, who hold the primary obligation of objecting to prejudicial evidence or conduct.... Certainly, the trial judge has an important gate-keeping function, but we cannot superimpose the role of defence counsel onto the trial judge.

Third, the trial judge's exercise of discretion in whether to admit evidence, to intervene, or permit certain conduct by the parties, deserves deference by appellate courts unless substantial wrong can be demonstrated.

Fourth, and finally, appellate courts must have faith in the intelligence and common sense of juries and in the ability of trial judges to properly charge juries.

A MATTER OF TIME

On the face of it, it would have seemed difficult to retry Trochym. The murder occurred in 1992. Trochym was charged and convicted of second-degree murder in 1995. He was sentenced to life in prison with no chance of parole for ten years. In 2007, the Supreme Court handed down its decision setting aside Trochym's conviction. Twelve years had passed between the first conviction and the Supreme Court decision, and fifteen years had passed since the murder itself.

A new trial was ordered. On August 14, 2009, Trochym, having proclaimed his innocence for seventeen years, pleaded not guilty to second-degree murder, but guilty to the lesser charge of manslaughter, citing his drunkenness at the time of the crime.

Justice Nola Garton sentenced Trochym to one day in jail and three years of probation. He had already served seven years and forty-eight days in pre-trial custody and jail.

HYPNOSIS: AN INVESTIGATIVE TOOL

Justice Deschamps stated in the Trochym case that hypnosis can be used as an investigative tool. She wrote:

> Some novel scientific techniques, such as polygraph examinations, that are inadmissible for evidentiary purposes [in criminal trials] may nevertheless continue to be useful for the investigation of offences. For example, while concerns about oath helping, character evidence and delay may prevent the use of polygraph results in court, these concerns do not preclude police officers from administering polygraph tests as an investigative tool.

CONSISTENT TESTIMONY

Assume that an accident victim believes that a red car struck her. Police, however, want greater certainty and, hopefully, greater detail. They ask the victim to undergo hypnosis, and she agrees. The result: The accident victim confirms her earlier story. She was struck by a red car.

At the trial of the alleged driver of the red car, no mention is made of hypnosis. However, defence counsel asks for more detail as to the identity of the car. The accident victim answers by giving the make, model, and year of the vehicle.

Should the testimony of the accident victim be allowed as to the identity of the car as being red? Justice Deschamps raised this hypothet in *Trochym*. She would not have permitted the testimony to be received. She wrote:

> Where evidence on topics covered during the hypnosis session is concerned, however, the trial judge should not admit it even if the witness did not change his or her testimony while under hypnosis. In my view, it would be inconsistent with the inadmissibility rule to allow those parts of the testimony, since they are tainted by the inherent shortcomings of the technique of hypnosis.
>
> Moreover, it would seem risky to take it for granted that the testimony at trial will be limited to pre-hypnosis memories. Indeed, the possibility that examination or cross-examination at trial will prompt answers more detailed than the recorded pre-hypnosis memories should not be underestimated....
>
> The overriding problem is that testimony on topics covered in a hypnosis session will be tainted. It will not cease to be tainted merely because it is consistent with a pre-hypnosis statement.

EDITORIAL COMMENT

The *Trochym* decision brought editorial comment from the *Globe and Mail* which stated in part:

> The issue of the general admissibility of post-hypnosis testimony didn't even arise in the 1992 murder case [*Trochym*] until it reached the [Ontario] Court of Appeal. The sole evidence advanced on the question, Judge Bastarache wrote, "was a handful of American cases in which the [state] courts have opted for categorical exclusion" of post-hypnosis testimony. The judges in the majority relied "almost exclusively on the position of experts discussed in American cases." The Crown didn't get a chance to present contrary evidence or to cross-examine the people identified as experts. [Justice Bastarache said,] "I have serious reservations about courts conducting personal research and forming conclusions on the basis of such research in areas that require expertise, like the sciences."
>
> While it would be invidious [offensive] to suggest that the majority on the Supreme Court was inventing policy on the fly, the six judges do appear to have bitten off more than they were reasonably in a position to chew. The issue of whether the fruits of hypnosis belong in the courtroom is a serious one, and the drawbacks of hypnosis may well outweigh the practice's probative value. But in all but rejecting its admissibility on so limited a basis of study, the court hasn't done the justice system any favours (*Globe and Mail,* June 2, 2007).

REFERENCES AND FURTHER READING

* Cited by the Supreme Court of Canada.

Bubela, Tania. "Expert Evidence: The Ethical Responsibility of the Legal Profession." *Alberta Law Review* 41 (2003–2004): 853.*

Cory, Peter deCarteret. *The Inquiry Regarding Thomas Sophonow: The Investigation, Prosecution and Consideration of Entitlement to Compensation.* Winnipeg: Manitoba Justice, 2001.*

Council on Scientific Affairs. "Scientific Status of Refreshing Recollection by the Use of Hypnosis." *Journal of the American Medical Association* 253 (1985): 1918.*

Daley, Beth. "Foolproof Forensics?" *Boston Globe,* June 8, 2004.

Diamond, Bernard L. "Inherent Problems in the Use of Pretrial Hypnosis on a Prospective Witness." *California Law Review* 68 (1980): 313.*

"Doctor Inquiry to Have Subpoena Power." *Canadian Press.* April 23, 2007.

Evans, Barrie K. "Hypnotically Induced Testimony: Implications for Criminal Law in New Zealand." *New Zealand Law Journal* 348 (1994).*

Frater, Robert J. "The Seven Deadly Prosecutorial Sins." *Canadian Criminal Law Review* 7 (2002): 209.*

Harset, Justin. "The Use of Hypnotically Enhanced Testimony in Criminal Trials." *Melbourne University Law Review* 20 (1996): 897.*

"Hypnosis on Trial." *Globe and Mail.* June 2, 2007.

McLean, Jesse. "After 17 Years, Stephen Trochym Admits Slaying." *Toronto Star,* August 15, 2009.

Ome, Martin T. "The Use and Misuse of Hypnosis in Court." 27 *International Journal of Clinical and Experimental Hypnosis* 27 (1979): 311.*

Perell, Paul M. "Proof of an Event of Which a Witness Has No Memory." *Advocates' Quarterly* 26 (2003): 95.*

Shaw, Gary M. "The Admissibility of Hypnotically Enhanced Testimony in Criminal Trials." *Marquette Law Review* 75 (1991): 1.*

Wagstaff, Graham F. "Hypnosis and the Law: A Critical Review of Some Recent Proposals." *Criminal Law Review* 152 (1983).*

Webert, Daniel R. "Are the Courts in a Trance? Approaches to the Admissibility of Hypnotically Enhanced Witness Testimony in Light of Empirical Evidence." *American Criminal Law Review* 40 (2003): 1301.*

CHAPTER 5

DNA TESTING: ANOTHER FORM OF SEARCH AND SEIZURE?

L aw sets the procedures for police to compel DNA samples in a crime scene investigation. Law also permits the Crown to introduce the results of DNA testing, and it allows courts to consider such results. The constitutionality of these laws, part of the Criminal Code, was considered in *S.A.B. v. The Queen and the Attorney General of Canada, Ontario, Quebec and New Brunswick*, decided by the Supreme Court on October 31, 2003. Justice Louise Arbour handed down the decision for a unanimous court. That ruling, which measures the law, part of the Criminal Code, against the Charter of Rights and Freedoms, forms an important part of this chapter.

Among the questions raised in this chapter are:

- What is DNA?
- How may DNA be used to fight crime?
- Can a person be compelled to give his/her body samples for DNA analysis?
- What is Canada's National DNA Bank?

There is no question that the forced taking of samples for DNA testing is a search and seizure within the meaning of law.

Police taking one's blood against that person's wishes is an invasion of personal privacy — even if it is in reasonable pursuit of a criminal investigation.

We will examine the constitutional limits placed on such action or, more precisely, the limits placed on police and courts under the Charter of Rights and Freedoms. In the S.A.B. case, the facts centred on whether the alleged offender impregnated a fourteen-year-old. She said he did, and the first step in identifying the offender was to establish the child's paternity.

It was at this point that police sought and obtained a warrant without hearing from the accused (called in law *ex parte*). It permitted them to compel him to give a blood sample which could be (and then was) used in evidence at his later trial for sexual assault and sexual exploitation. The facts will be developed more fully in the discussion that follows.

We will follow and somewhat expand upon the path taken by Justice Arbour in setting out the decision of the Court. That path was intended to establish the statutory background for the forced taking of DNA samples. This provides a context, Justice Arbour stated, for determining whether the forced search and seizure was "reasonable" within the meaning of section 8 of the Charter which provides: "Everyone has the right to be secure against unreasonable search and seizure."

We will go beyond the path set by Justice Arbour by providing a more in-depth look at the nature of Canada's National DNA Bank, which was only briefly mentioned by Justice Arbour. That facility, referred to as NDDB, is an ongoing depository for DNA samples from repeat convicted offenders of violent and sexual crimes. We will describe the "success" of the NDDB in its "hit" score of matched DNA.

As well, through "You Be the Judge" and "Challenge Questions," we will raise related Charter issues. The most important, perhaps, is the extent to which the right against self-incrimination trumps any Crown right for warrants to compel search and seizure of

DNA samples.

Yet, the start point properly is one of defining the nature of DNA and its role in criminal investigations. In that regard, it is well to state the extent to which DNA analysis is the same as, or goes beyond, the historical investigatory tool of fingerprinting.

DNA DEFINED

Deoxyribonucleic acid (DNA) is a long, double-stranded molecule that looks like a twisted rope ladder or double helix. Sometimes referred to as the blueprint of life, DNA is the fundamental building block for one's entire genetic makeup.

An individual's DNA results when sperm and egg unite. The result is equal amounts of DNA from that person's mother and father. DNA is found in every tissue in the human body. The DNA in the blood is the same as the DNA in the skin cells, saliva, and the roots of one's hair.

With the exception of identical twins, each person's DNA is unique. As such, DNA is a powerful tool for identifying individuals.

TESTING

DNA can be taken from a small biological sample, such as a few drops of blood. This sample can be analyzed and used to create a unique and individual DNA profile. In many ways, it is like a genetic fingerprint. A DNA profile, drawn from a known biological sample, can be compared to other DNA profiles stored in a data bank.

If a profile match results, the two samples likely come from the same person. If the profiles don't match, the samples likely come from different people. The word "likely" means that scientists can put the outcome of the comparisons in terms of odds of the same outcome with a different person. (This was the thrust of the experts' testimony in the S.A.B. case, discussed below.)

The DNA molecule is very stable. It is difficult to destroy. This means that scientists can get new information from old biological evidence or from otherwise damaged samples, such as clothing. The stability of the molecule, combined with the unique features of each person's DNA and the accuracy of current DNA analysis techniques, makes this human identification technology an important part of many police investigations.

HAIR: NEW EVIDENCE?

Consider the appeal in 2013 of the first-degree murder conviction of Leighton Hay. He was charged with the shooting death in 2002 of Colin Moore, a respected community figure, at a Toronto nightclub where a community fundraiser was being held. Hay had served ten years of a life sentence. The Association in Defence of the Wrongly Convicted took Hay's appeal, which related to new forensic evidence that Hay's lawyers claimed would prove Hay's innocence — hair samples.

In an unusual move, the Supreme Court, in a 7–0 decision, ruled that a new trial was necessary to consider the "fresh evidence." Justice Rothstein, speaking for the Court, said the new evidence "could reasonably be expected to have affected the jury's verdict.... The interests of justice require that the Court remit the matter for a new trial, in which the Crown would have the opportunity to adduce evidence challenging the reliability of the fresh evidence."

THE FACTS

The Crown presented evidence that Hay and Gary Eunick shot Moore several times in a dispute over paying a cover charge after arriving at the club after midnight. Eunick was identified by multiple witnesses. Hay was identified by just one witness — and that witness said that a two-year-old photo looked 80 percent like him.

The evidence against Hay rested in hair found in Hay's

bathroom garbage, as well as hair found in Hay's electric razor. The Crown prosecutor argued that Hay had shaved his scalp to change his appearance and prevent identification by witnesses.

Both men were convicted on first-degree murder.

Hay, through his lawyers, had the hair tested and, through experts, obtained opinions that the samples did not come from his scalp. The Court stated: "Mr. Hay argues that the fresh evidence establishes that the hair clippings did not come from a shave of Mr. Hay's scalp and that, as a result, acquittal or a new trial is warranted."

The Supreme Court ruling overturned the decision of the Ontario Court of Appeal.

A FORM OF FINGERPRINTING?

Is DNA testing just another form of fingerprinting? Fingerprinting can do no more than disclose similarities between one set of prints and another. The results of DNA testing can go far beyond those of fingerprinting.

It is possible through DNA testing to get a physical and even a limited snapshot of the emotional makeup of an individual. For example, this picture can include gender, hair colour, whether the person is right-handed or left-handed, and the likelihood of genetic diseases. Further, in one type of DNA testing (mitochondrial) it is even possible to determine whether such characteristics have been passed from a mother to her children. In 1996, the FBI in the United States set up a lab to do this more complete testing.

DNA USES BEYOND CRIMINAL LAW: SOME POSSIBLE CASES

The S.A.B. case was a criminal proceeding involving the paternity of the fetus as a key element of evidence. DNA testing was central to resolving that question. Paternity, of course, can determine civil liability — that is, whether an individual is the father and, as such, bears responsibility for the support of the child. That same determination of parentage can aid in resolving claims to the estate of a deceased person (i.e. genetic relationship).

TORT ACTIONS

Genetic information could be used as evidence in various tort (usually negligence) actions, including those for personal injury, medical negligence, or product liability. For example, in the United States, wrongful life and wrongful birth cases have been brought for failure to inform patients of the risks of having children with serious genetic disorders, and for the negligent administration of tests for genetic diseases.

The legal elements of a claim in negligence often are that the defendant owed the plaintiff a duty of care; the defendant breached that duty; and the plaintiff suffered damage that was caused by the breach of the duty and was not too remote from it in law. Where negligence is established, the court may award damages to the plaintiff.

It has been said that, in the past, the tort system, with some exceptions, has treated all persons as identical. Generally there has been no basis for isolating individual risk factors from the risk posed to the general population. Now, however, there are a number of ways in which genetic information and, in particular, genetic test results could potentially be applied by courts in tort actions.

A defendant in a negligence action may use genetic information to disprove the plaintiff's charge that he or she caused the plaintiff's injury. For example, where a plaintiff had a genetic predisposition to the same condition that he or she ultimately developed, the defendant could argue that it was the predisposition, rather than the defendant, that caused the injury. Alternatively, a defendant might argue that the predisposition was a contributing cause of the injury in order to minimize his or her own liability.

PALM PRINTS: BEYOND FINGERPRINTS — BETTER THAN DNA?

Law enforcement officers and prosecutors have moved to another form of fingerprinting: *palm prints.* Police estimate that 30 percent of prints lifted at crime scenes (for example, from knife hilts, gun grips, steering wheels, and window panes) are of palms, not fingers. By "palms" we mean all of the "friction ridged skin" on a person's hands. These patterns, unique to all individuals, are found on the soles, palms, and even the writer's palm, as the outer side of the hand is called.

In April 2003, the New York City Police began having prisoners place their whole hand, not just their fingertips, on the glass platen of a scanner when their prints are captured. Since December 2003, the department has been able to do computerized matches of the one hundred thousand palm prints it has already collected. As the database grows, it will become one of the largest of its kind. The cost to upgrade the existing police archive, digitize the palm prints, and purchase additional scanners is estimated at $11.7 million (U.S.).

The palm print database already has been put to use. Three people were murdered in 2001 in an apartment over the Carnegie Deli, a popular restaurant in Manhattan. Police ran a check on one suspect and learned he had been arrested in Georgia. The palm print card from that arrest was carried to New York by a special courier. It matched a palm print found on duct tape used to bind the victims.

FIGHTING CRIME: TECHNOLOGY'S LIMITS

Palm print and DNA testing have broadened the scope of crime investigation. But, there are limits to the effectiveness of technology in law enforcement. Not the least of these limits is the need for police to be aware that crime has been committed. They would have difficulty bringing their forensic tools to bear in the absence of a belief that there has been a crime.

Consider those who kill by poison. In 2003, Charles Cullen, a New Jersey nurse, admitted to killing a number of patients with drug overdoses during his sixteen-year career. It was a career which included five job discharges related, at least in part, to the mishandling of lethal drugs and suspicions (but no more than that) regarding some patient deaths.

Mark Essig, an author, wrote:

> Thanks to chromatography and later developments like mass spectrometry and immunoassay, even tiny amounts of a poison, absorbed into the blood and distributed throughout the body, can now be separated out. It is a simple matter to detect digoxin, the heart medication that Mr. Cullen allegedly used to kill a New Jersey priest and several others.
>
> But before toxicologists can find evidence of poison, they have to be asked to look for it. The best science in the world can't detect a crime unless someone first suspects that a crime took place. Because the medical profession lacks adequate [and practical] standards for reporting complaints against nurses, Mr. Cullen was able to hop from job to job, obscuring an alarming pattern of behavior. It should now be clear that both state licensing boards and the federal National Practitioner Database — created in 1990 to track troubled doctors and nurses — must take their responsibilities more seriously (*New York Times*, January 4, 2003).

CHALLENGE QUESTION

WITHOUT A BODY, HOW CAN MURDER BE PROVED?

A family of three disappears. Mother, father, and child have not been seen for several days. Mail and newspapers have accumulated. Some of the neighbours are concerned and call police, who visit the home and find the door unlocked. The inside of the home is strewn with overturned furniture, and there appears to be blood spots on the floor. An "amber" alert call goes out for the child, and officers are asked to find the parents as well.

A search is conducted in the neighbourhood, the city, the province, nationally, and even internationally. All those who had any contact with the family are asked to co-operate and, for the most part, they do. The family cannot be found.

Believing that the home of the family might be a crime scene, police obtain the proper authorization to conduct a detailed search. They find a few strands of hair on a living room chair. Checking that hair against specimens filed with a national DNA bank of convicted felons, police find a match. The hair appears to be from a felon previously convicted of aggravated assault. He resides in the area of the family home.

Police believe that, at the very least, they have is a "person of interest." They consult with the crown prosecutor: Suppose, they ask, that the family cannot be found — that they are dead.

Q. Would it be possible to bring murder charges against the "person of interest" — to name him as the accused? Can murder charges be laid without a body?

Yes. David Butt, a Toronto-based criminal lawyer and former prosecutor, said that with comprehensive police investigation laying the foundation of the case, it is not impossible to prosecute a first degree murder case without a body having been found and examined. Indeed, Butt is one of the few lawyers in Canada who has successfully prosecuted a first degree murder case without a body of the victim having been found.

Butt said that that there are three "ideas" necessary for an effective prosecution:

1. Almost without exception, murder trials are heard by a jury of twelve persons who, in making their decision, draw on the evidence filtered through their own life experiences. The goal, quite simply, is to provide an explanation for both the crime and the missing remains that makes sense.

2. Next, the prosecutor must tap the powerful tool of circumstantial evidence. "Circumstantial evidence," said Butt, "is simply a matter of proving what we cannot see. We do this all the time."

3. Finally, the prosecutor must demonstrate that there are no reasonable alternative explanations for the absence of a body. Butt said that silence after a disappearance — i.e. no ransom demand — can mean that "murder is staring at you in the face" (*Globe and Mail*, July 15, 2014).

THE BIRTH OF DNA EVIDENCE — INNOCENCE AND GUILT

In 1983, a fifteen-year-old girl was found raped and murdered along a lonely footpath called Black Pad that separated a cemetery from a psychiatric hospital in the British village of Narborough in Leicestershire. For the police, however, this murder was different. The murderer had left his genetic identity in seminal stains found on the victim's body and clothing.

About three years later, another fifteen-year-old was raped and murdered. Her body was found on a footpath in the village of Enderby, a short distance from the first murder scene. Again, seminal stains were found on the clothing and the body of the victim.

The serological protein forensic test developed from seminal stains identified the contributor as having the phosphoglucomutase (PGM+1) secretor A status that matched the first victim's killer profile. This is found in approximately 10 percent of the male population of Britain.

ARRESTED AND FREED

A major investigation quickly resulted in the arrest of a young kitchen porter who was charged with the second murder. For police, the question then seemed to be whether the porter also was responsible for the first murder.

In an attempt to solve both murders and link the biological evidence, a new test soon to be known as "DNA fingerprinting" was applied by Dr. Alec Jeffreys, the scientist who had developed the procedure. When the test was completed, Dr. Jeffreys had exonerated an innocent man (the prime suspect) as well as linked both murders through an identical genetic signature. On November 21, 1986, in the Crown Court of Leicester, the young kitchen porter made legal history as the first person to be exonerated from a crime through the use of genetic evidence.

FINDING THE MURDERER

One year later, Colin Pitchfork was arrested and later found guilty of the rape and the murder of both girls. After an extensive investigation and the comparison of 4,583 genetic profiles of male residents in the surrounding villages, Dr. Jeffrey's test had matched the genetic profile to one person.

In 1988, Pitchfork was sentenced to life for the two murders and he became the first person to be convicted for murder based on genetic fingerprinting, known in North America as DNA typing.

THE QUEEN V. S.A.B. — DNA WARRANTS

Now we come to the Criminal Code provisions for issuing DNA warrants, which are court orders to compel taking DNA samples for testing and possible use in trials. It was here that Justice Arbour, speaking for the Supreme Court of Canada, chose to begin her analysis of *The Queen v. S.A.B.*

The approach of the Court was to point out those legislative provisions designed to both protect the individual against what section 8 of the Charter prohibits — unreasonable search and seizure — and the interest of the state in finding the truth as to the commission of a crime. (Yet, it remained to be seen whether the requirements of the Charter had been satisfied, whatever might have been the intent of the Parliament. That will bring us to the second part of Justice Arbour's analysis.)

This is what the Criminal Code provides as to the issuance of DNA warrants:

1. Such warrants can be issued allowing only the Crown to be heard, without affording the person from whom the DNA sample is to be taken the right to question the warrant. (This is called an *ex parte* hearing.) The reason for not allowing

a full hearing is that the Parliament sensed the individual from whom the DNA sample would be taken, if notified in advance, might flee.

2. However, this does not mean an absence of a hearing. The law enforcement officers must come with a sworn statement (called an *affidavit*) before a provincial court judge (a more elevated position than that of what had been a justice of the peace). The officer(s) there must convince the judge that there are reasonable grounds to believe that one of the specifically listed offences in the Criminal Code (primarily serious violent and sexual offences) has been committed (Criminal Code, section 487.04).

3. Further, the affidavit of the officers must show that a "bodily substance" was found in the victim or near that person; that the person named in the affidavit was a "party" to the offence; and that the DNA analysis sought will show whether the bodily substance sought was from the individual named in the warrant.

4. Even bearing in mind these conditions, the judge is given further discretion under the Criminal Code. The judge must be satisfied that the issuance of a DNA warrant is in the best interests of the administration of justice (Criminal Code, section 487.05(1)). In this regard, the judge must consider the nature of the claimed offence and the circumstances of its alleged commission, and whether the law officer named to take the DNA sample has, in fact, the training and experience to do so (Criminal Code, section 487.05(2)). It should be noted that the law officer is given permission under the law to seek the DNA warrant by telephone, fax, or e-mail when that officer believes it would be "impractical to appear personally before a judge (Criminal Code, section 487.05(3))."

(Note: For all this, the law will allow the judge to order a *full* hearing with representation by the person from whom the DNA sample is sought. This may be done where the judge believes the interest in the administration of justice so requires.)

5. The DNA warrant is no blanket permission to extract blood or, for example, hair samples. The Criminal Code designates what may be done in this regard, such as plucking individual hairs, swabbing the lips, tongue and inside cheeks and mouth (buccal swabs), and taking blood by pricking the skin surface with a sterile lancet (Criminal Code, section 487.06(1)).

6. The DNA warrant must be served on the individual subject to the test. The warrant must state the procedure for taking such samples; the purpose of the DNA tests, and the authority to use as much force as necessary to take the designated tests. If the individual subject to the warrant is a young person, there is the right to have counsel (or a parent, or a friend) present at the time the test samples are taken. The young person may waive his/her rights for such representation but, to do so, the waiver must be in writing (signed), or by audio or video.

THE USE OF THE SEIZED DNA MATERIALS

A DNA sample could allow for disclosure of an individual's biological, medical, or even genetically rooted emotional characteristics. But, such information is specifically denied to law enforcement officers in seeking and carrying out DNA tests. Their statutory authority is limited to forensic DNA analysis. Under the statute, this means only the "comparison of the DNA of the bodily substance from a person in execution of a warrant with the results of the DNA in the bodily substance" of that resulting from the DNA test.

The test may be used only for the purpose of determining if there is a "match" between the sample taken at the crime scene and that taken under the DNA warrant. Its use is strictly limited to this narrow sphere of law enforcement, nothing more. To do otherwise would result in a crime punishable as an offence on summary conviction (Criminal Code, section 487.08(3)).

Indeed, the test results are to be destroyed by the state: (a) if the results are negative, that is, they do not match; (b) if the person is acquitted of the offence charged; or (c) at the end of a year, if there is a discharge following a preliminary hearing, or a withdrawal of the information on which the charges were based. (Destruction is also ordered under the law on the same circumstances if the test DNA sample was provided voluntarily.)

THE CHARTER APPLIED TO THE FACTS AND THE CRIMINAL CODE

Justice Arbour addressed herself to the application of the Charter to the facts and the provisions of the Criminal Code cited. Based on the facts, she found that S.A.B. was charged with sexual assault and sexual exploitation of a fourteen-year-old under sections 271 and 153(1)(a) of the Criminal Code.

The charges stemmed from incidents that allegedly took place in Hinton, Alberta, around July 1996. (Note: The decision of the Supreme Court of Canada was handed down on October 31, 2003 — seven years after the claimed incidents.) A few months following the asserted sexual assault, the fourteen-year-old discovered that she was pregnant. She told her mother that S.A.B., who had been living with the family for several months, had sexually assaulted her. She had an abortion and the police seized the fetal tissue.

The police then obtained an *ex parte* DNA warrant to compel a blood sample from S.A.B. Typically, a forensic DNA analysis will compare two samples of DNA to determine if they match. In this case, however, the DNA analysis compared S.A.B.'s blood sample with the fetal tissue (the combined DNA of the fourteen-year-old and S.A.B.) taken from the fourteen-year-old's body to confirm or deny that S.A.B. had fathered the fetus. In effect, this was a paternity test. The results of that test led to S.A.B. being charged as indicated.

At trial, evidence was given by the DNA expert that five of the seven DNA samples taken from S.A.B. were "conclusive and established the probability that S.A.B. was not the father of the fetus to be *one in ten million* [emphasis added]." The expert further testified that the sixth test sample was damaged and yielded inconclusive results. The seventh sample, the expert continued, did not match; it was a "mutation." According to so-called international standards, if there had been a second mutation, then the conclusion would have to be that S.A.B. was not the father. This did not happen, and there was no question raised concerning the so-called "international standards."

THE SUPREME COURT RULES

Having stated the facts, and summarized relevant provisions of the law relating to *ex parte* DNA warrants, Justice Arbour then applied section 8 of the Charter which prohibits unreasonable search and seizure. Speaking for a unanimous Court, she ruled that both the statute and its application were in compliance with the Charter. She stated:

> The taking of bodily samples under a DNA warrant clearly interferes with bodily integrity. However, under a properly issued DNA warrant, the degree of offence to the physical integrity of the person is relatively modest.... A buccal [inside the mouth] swab is quick and not terribly intrusive. Blood samples are obtained by pricking the surface of the skin — a procedure that is, as conceded by [S.A.B.], not particularly invasive in the physical sense. With the exception of pubic hair, the plucking of hairs should not be a particularly serious affront to privacy or dignity.
>
> Importantly, §487.07(3) of the legislation [Criminal Code] requires that the person who is

authorized to take samples do so in a manner that respects the offender's privacy and is "reasonable in the circumstances."

Section 487.06(2) additionally provides that the warrant "shall include any terms and conditions that the provincial court judge considers advisable to ensure that the seizure of a bodily substance authorized by the warrant is reasonable in the circumstances."

In my view, the statutory framework alleviates any concern that the collection of DNA samples pursuant to a search warrant under §§487.04 to 487.09 of the Criminal Code constitutes an intolerable affront to the physical integrity of the person.

The informational aspect of privacy is also clearly engaged by the taking of bodily samples for the purposes of executing a DNA warrant. In fact, this is the central concern involved in the collection of DNA information by the state. Privacy in relation to information derives from the assumption that all information about a person is in a fundamental way his or her own, to be communicated or retained by the individual in question as he or she sees fit.... There is undoubtedly the highest level of personal and private information contained in an individual's DNA. However, it is important to recall that the bodily samples collected pursuant to a search warrant issued under §§487.04 to 487.09 are collected for a limited purpose, clearly articulated in the Criminal Code.

The DNA warrant scheme limits the intrusion into informational privacy by using only non-coding DNA for forensic DNA analysis. As previously noted, s. 487.04 defines "forensic DNA analysis"

as the comparison of the DNA in the bodily substance seized from a person in execution of a warrant with the results of the DNA in the bodily substance referred to in §487.05(1)(b). *In other words,
the DNA analysis is conducted solely for forensic
purposes and does not reveal any medical, physical
or mental characteristics; its only use is the provision
of identifying information that can be compared to
an existing sample* [emphasis added].

Additional factors limit the intrusion into informational privacy: §487.05(1)(b), §487.08(1) and
§487.08(2) place limits on the use of the information obtained from DNA analysis including making it an offence to use a bodily substance obtained
in execution of a DNA warrant except in the course
of an investigation of the designated offence. That
the DNA warrant scheme explicitly prohibits the
misuse of information is an important factor that
ensures compliance with §8 of the Charter.

It is also necessary to consider the interests
of the state in seeking a DNA warrant. The state's
interest in the DNA warrant scheme is a significant
one. Effective law enforcement benefits society as
a whole. Subsumed under the larger head of "law
enforcement" is the interest in arriving at the truth
in order to bring offenders to justice and to avoid
wrongful convictions. The enormous utility and
power of DNA evidence as an investigative tool
has been documented both by trial judge[s] and
by the Ontario Court of Appeal.... Indeed, "a DNA
match will in many cases, with virtual certainty,
eliminate the person as a suspect ... [or] provide
evidence that it was his bodily substance(s) that
was found at one or more of the places set out in

§487.05(1)(b)".... This is an identification tool of great value to the criminal process.

I can therefore conclude that, in general terms, the DNA warrant provisions of the Criminal Code strike an appropriate balance between the public interest in effective criminal law enforcement for serious offences, and the rights of individuals to control the release of personal information about themselves, as well as their right to dignity and physical integrity.

A CANADIAN DNA DATABASE

In 2000, about eleven years after the RCMP first began to use DNA testing, a Canadian national DNA database was established. At the time, other DNA databases existed in the U.S., Germany, Britain, Norway, Finland, Belgium, and Denmark. However, Canada's database (which cost an initial ten million dollars and is housed in RCMP headquarters in Ottawa) is somewhat unique, according to Dr. Ron Fourney, who was then in charge of the program. At an estimated annual operating cost of five million dollars, Dr. Fourney said that there is heavy reliance on robotics in processing, developing, and comparing DNA profiles.

At the time of establishment of the database, it was projected that each DNA test would take about five days to process. Police estimated that thirty thousand samples from known serious offenders, suspected criminals, and crime scenes would be processed annually. Dr. Fourney said: "When we started ten years ago, we might have needed a biological sample which was the size of a penny. Today's technology is so revolutionary that 10 percent of what would fit on the head of a pin is all we'd need to do a case."

DNA AT BIRTH?

Some law enforcement officials in the U.S. have suggested the establishment of a national DNA bank for all residents. DNA would be taken at birth, and it would be used exclusively for criminal investigations (*New York Times*, January 4, 2003).

OF DRAGNETS AND "VOLUNTEERS" — AND INTERNATIONAL AGREEMENTS

In the cases of the two murdered girls — described in "The Birth of DNA Evidence — Innocence and Guilt" — British police, in effect, conducted a "dragnet" of males living in the area near the crime scenes. They asked for — and got — genetic samples from 4,583 men. The samples were given "voluntarily" (though any refusal might well have been met by publicity). One of the samples, as noted, resulted in a "match." That person was charged with the two murders and found guilty.

Suppose the same kind of dragnet were initiated by police in Canada. Would police be able to take the samples of those that had *not* matched and place them in a data bank for later possible matching in other crimes? Could police share such information with law enforcement officers in other nations?

The answer is no to both questions, but with a caution as to the second.

Section 487.05(1)(b) of the Criminal Code states that bodily substances provided voluntarily by a person, and the results of the DNA analysis, are to be destroyed without delay if there is no match in terms of that being investigated. In addition, removal is required if the results are put into electronic form.

It is unclear as to how such testing results can be destroyed once they are "shared" with other nations. Of course, the problem is limited if member nations subject to agreements stipulate that they will use information supplied by Canada only as permitted by Canadian law. As noted, DNA databases already exist in a number of other countries. Canada has negotiated and entered agreements with other nations that possess DNA databanks to set up a system where genetic information can be exchanged. Officials of the Canada National Data Bank in their website have stated:

> As an additional safeguard, plus an important transparent link to the public, the National DNA Data Bank Advisory Committee was appointed by the Solicitor General of Canada in early 2000 to function as an independent body to oversee the effectiveness and efficiency of the National DNA Data Bank. The Committee was established pursuant to the DNA Identification Act and the annexed Data Bank Advisory Committee Regulations and is charged to report to the Commissioner of the RCMP annually.
>
> Since the inauguration of the Committee and the opening of the Data Bank in June 2000, members have regularly reviewed all aspects of the implementation process and the Data Bank operations. *Particular attention has been directed to the interrelationships between the Crime Scene Index and the Convicted Offenders Index. As well, the DNA Data Bank will be subject to auditing by the Office of the Privacy Commissioner at any time.* Also, a representative of the Privacy Commissioner sits on the DNA Data Bank Advisory Committee to ensure that the Data Bank has available expert advice in the field of individual privacy [emphasis added].
>
> The DNA Identification Act provides for criminal penalties for anyone communicating

information relating to the biological samples being analyzed or retained, and penalties for using the data derived from the analysis for any purpose other than that intended. It is very clear in the Act that the DNA Data Bank is a post-conviction data bank providing an investigative tool for law enforcement purposes only.

The same standards that apply to the use of DNA profiles in Canada will govern international exchanges with other criminal justice organizations. There is provision for cooperation with other jurisdictions in the use of this valuable investigative tool. Such interaction, however, must be sanctioned by international agreements that clearly define the conditions under which DNA profile data may be exchanged.

A COMMON STANDARD

The Combined DNA Index System (CODIS) is the North American accepted standard for DNA profile data that allows for reliable and valid electronic transmission in a secure format. The FBI and the U.S. Department of Justice provide the software at no charge to any law enforcement agency performing the DNA profiling procedure which follows a similar code of quality assurance and justice. Once the DNA profile is appropriately formatted, it is uploaded to CODIS from the Convicted Offender Index.

THE CANADIAN NATIONAL DNA DATA BANK

The Criminal Code contains two sets of provisions dealing with the collection and use of DNA evidence. The first, which was the subject of the S.A.B. case, relates to search and seizure of DNA evidence in the course of an investigation. The second deals with the collection of DNA evidence from convicted persons for inclusion in the National DNA Data Bank (NDDB). (See, Criminal Code, sections 487.051–487.058, 487.071, and 487.091. These provisions should be read along with the DNA Identification Act, *Statutes of Canada*, 1998, chapter 37.) There is, however, a connection between the two sets of laws

The NDDB has provisions designed to protect, up to a point, DNA privacy concerns. These conditions are specified in the DNA Identification Act. As noted, there are two indices maintained by the NDDB. The first is the Convicted Offenders Index (COI). For this index, biological samples resulting in DNA profiles can be collected only from convicted offenders and they can only be used for law enforcement purposes. They can't be used, for example, to develop a medical profile of the individual. Further, the class of convicted offenders from whom samples for DNA purposes can be extracted is limited to those found guilty of violent and/or sexual offences such as murder, attempted murder, sexual assault, assault, breaking and entering with intent (and breaking out), and armed robbery. Those on this list are fingerprinted for identification. Their prints and their DNA profiles are then digitally stored. Once they are properly included on this index, they remain there for the rest of the lives of the persons tested.

The second grouping , called the Crime Scene Index (CSI), is a separate electronic index composed of DNA profiles resulting from crime scene investigations of the offences listed above. The discussion in *S.A.B.* sets out the conditions both for requiring DNA profiles and, once obtained, when they must be removed from the data bank.

As seen by the NDDB, the purposes of the indices are:

- to link crimes together where there are no suspects;
- to identify suspects;

- to eliminate suspects where there is no match between crime scene DNA and a DNA profile in the NDDB; and
- to determine whether a serial offender is involved.

THE PROCESS FOR DNA FOLLOWING A CONVICTION

At the time a sample is collected from a convicted offender, a unique number or "bar code" is attached. It remains the sole identifier throughout the analysis process so that the personal identity of the donor is not known to the DNA Data Bank staff.

When the collected samples are first received at the NDDB, the fingerprints on the sample collection card and the fingerprint identification form are compared to ensure that they match. This is an important first step which confirms the Data Bank information. After this confirmation of match, the biological sample is separated from the information contained on the fingerprint identification form. The fingerprint identification form and the documentation are then forwarded to the Canadian Criminal Records Information Service (CCRIS) within the RCMP's Information and Identification Services Directorate.

The biological sample card, identified solely by its bar code, is transferred to the NDDB laboratory for analysis. Upon successful completion of the DNA profiling process, a "flag" (which states "DNA on known offender Data Bank") is placed on the offender's record to indicate that the offender has a reliable DNA profile entered into the COI. This is primarily provided as an easy reference check so that police officers or prosecutors may, under section 487.053 of the Criminal Code, advise the court that there is already a DNA profile belonging to the offender in the DNA Data Bank.

If the DNA profile from a crime scene sample (analyzed by one of the operational forensic laboratories) matches the DNA profile from a convicted offender sample, the submitting laboratory is contacted by CCRIS and can then associate the crime scene sample with an individual.

When a match in the Crime Scene Index is found between two crime scene profiles, the submitting laboratories are notified. The identity of the donor or the specific nature of the biological sample (blood, hair, etc.) are not known to the staff of the DNA Data Bank. However, the operational forensic laboratories which originally submitted the DNA profile data from the crime scenes can now exchange information, linking the crime scenes.

PRIVACY CONCERNS

The question of privacy is dealt with in the following ways by the NDDB:

1. Scientific processes: The DNA analysis process used by the Data Bank examines only a small segment of the entire human DNA blueprint which encodes anonymous pieces of DNA. Apart from the ability to identify gender, there is no known link to physical or medical attributes.

2. Methodology: By design, the genetic and personal data are separated. The Data Bank will have the DNA profile and original biological sample, but the personal information and full set of fingerprints of convicted offenders are in the custody of the Canadian Criminal Records Information Service (CCRIS), and are retained under strict security provisions.

3. Physical limits: It will not be possible for unauthorized persons to enter the Data Bank and view or retrieve data. In order to be able to interpret the data, specialized knowledge is required. For genetic DNA data to be linked to an individual, access to two separate and secure data bases, housed in separate locations, would be required.

4. Legal: The act specifies criminal penalties for unauthorized use of the DNA profile data or the samples themselves.

CHALLENGE QUESTION

THE "LAST RESORT" TEST

Court warrants — that is, authorization for law enforcement officers to intercept and record private communications — are ordered only if other investigative means have been tried and failed, or are not likely to succeed. These are requirements of section 186(1)(b) of the Criminal Code. They are also requirements of the Charter. (See, *R. v. Araujo*, [2000] 2 *Supreme Court of Canada Reports* 992.)

Such conditions are a "last resort" investigative tool. This means that, among other things, the burden is on the Crown to show that other investigative means are not available to it.

Q. To what extent, if any, should DNA warrants be subject to the wiretap rule of "last resort"?

Justice Arbour, speaking for the Supreme Court of Canada in *S.A.B.*, refused to apply the "last resort" test to DNA warrants. There are, she said, real differences between wiretaps and DNA testing. In a wiretap, the police hear all that is spoken. No lines are drawn as to the communication itself. In DNA testing, the process is only concerned with whether there is a match with a known sample taken from the crime scene. Justice Arbour wrote:

> I see no reason to import, as a constitutional imperative, a similar requirement in the case of DNA warrants. There are obvious differences between the use of wiretaps

as an investigative tool, and recourse to a DNA warrant.

Wiretaps are sweeping in their reach. They invariably intrude into the privacy interests of third parties who are not targeted by the criminal investigation. They cast a net that is inevitably wide. By contrast, DNA warrants are target specific. Significantly, DNA warrants also have the capacity to exonerate an accused early in the investigative process.

CHALLENGE QUESTIONS

OF STRIP SEARCHES AND DNA WARRANTS

Q. Isn't a warrant commanding the taking of a person's DNA similar to a strip search? If so, then isn't the standard for granting such a warrant placed at a higher level?

These were questions raised by defence counsel in *S.A.B.* and Justice Arbour, for the Court, rejected the challenges. She stated that strip searches have been found by the Court to be "inherently humiliating and degrading." But, such searches are permitted under the law, subject to the same standard as any other search, namely, reasonable grounds.

Whether reasonable grounds exist must be related to the facts of the case. Taking a blood sample or a bit of hair, Justice Arbour said, is not the same as forcing a person to strip and initiating a body cavity search. She wrote:

> The [defendant's] second concern is that the standard of "reasonable grounds" alone, which is appropriate for ordinary warrants, is insufficient for searches and seizures that violate bodily integrity and force self-conscription. In my view, this exaggerates the degree of intrusiveness of DNA warrants. With respect to the concerns for personal dignity and bodily integrity, the proper execution of a DNA warrant would compare favourably to strip searches.... Strip searches [have been] held to be "inherently humiliating and degrading," but nonetheless valid, provided certain conditions were met, when conducted on the basis of a reasonable and probable grounds standard. The standard of "reasonable grounds" is well recognized in the law and I see no reason to adopt a higher one in the case of DNA warrants.

YOU BE THE JUDGE

A MATTER OF SELF-INCRIMINATION?

The issue in this case is real. It was raised in *S.A.B.*

THE FACTS

On the night of June 4, 2003, on a dimly lit street in Vancouver, Oscar, the victim, was struck on the head several times with a heavy, blunt instrument. It seemed clear to police forensic experts that Oscar tried to fight off his assailant. Splattered blood — some of which did not match Oscar's blood type — was found at the crime scene. In addition, some hair follicles not belonging to Oscar were found. Oscar fell into a coma from which it is uncertain that he will regain consciousness. No one came forward who might have witnessed the assault.

Within hours of the assault, police learned that David, a person long known to them and convicted of several assaults in the past, was identified as being in the area at the time. The police wanted a DNA warrant to test David's blood, and to take a hair sample from him for DNA analysis. The investigating officers came before a provincial judge to obtain such an order. They did this without informing David of their request. (This is called an *ex parte* hearing.)

The law under which the police have acted is the same as in *S.A.B.* David, however, refused to submit to a blood sample or to allow anyone to take any hair from him.

THE ISSUE

May David claim the right against self-incrimination to justify his refusal to give blood and hair samples for DNA analysis?

POINTS TO CONSIDER

- Sections 487.04–487.09 of the Criminal Code, as described in *S.A.B.*, clearly allow a judge to grant a warrant based on police sworn statements (*affidavits*) that show a relationship between the DNA sought and their investigation of a specific crime.
- It is also clear, as applied to David, that the necessary relationship exists for such a DNA warrant.
- The principle against self-incrimination is basic to many of those rights afforded by the Charter. That right is based on the individual not being forced to give evidence against himself/herself to support any charges brought by the police or to aid the Crown's prosecution of that person.
- The principle against self-incrimination finds expression in several provisions of the Charter. For example, section 8 of the Charter, as was pointed out in the discussion of *S.A.B.*, provides that "everyone has the right to be secure against unreasonable search and seizure." In effect, the individual is made secure from the state taking him/her (or his/her property) on unreasonable grounds.
- Also, section 11(c) of the Charter states that "any person charged with an offence has the right not to be compelled to be a witness in proceedings against that person in respect of the offence."

DISCUSSION

The right against self-incrimination is an important value within the Charter, said Justice Arbour in *S.A.B.* But, it is a right that is subject to reasonable restraints. That which is reasonable must be judged on the facts in the context of the interests of the individual and those of the state.

Those interests may be characterized as: (1) protecting against unreliable confessions; and (2) protecting against the abuse of state power. Confessions (evidence) obtained by force may not be truthful. They may be given to satisfy the perceived sense of what the law enforcement office wants rather than the truth as to what actually happened. And, bearing in mind that ours is a free society with rights constitutionally entrenched, there is a need for courts to help guard against an abuse of power by the state. It is the state that must prove the defendant violated the law.

Viewing the interests of S.A.B. and taking a bit of blood from him as against the interests of the state in seeking the truth as to the paternity of the foetus, Justice Arbour had little difficulty in denying any claim to the right against self-incrimination under the Charter. The same result likely would come from the facts relating to David.

THE SUPREME COURT SPEAKS IN *S.A.B.*
Justice Arbour, speaking for the Supreme Court of Canada in *S.A.B.*, wrote:

> Not all conscriptive [required] evidence will violate the principle against self-incrimination. Indeed, that principle has

a limited scope, and requires different things at different times.

As this Court recognized ... the principle against self-incrimination rests on the fundamental notion that the Crown has the burden of establishing a "case to meet" and must do so without the compelled participation of the accused.

The question, then, is whether the DNA warrant provisions at issue in this case impermissibly violate the principle against self-incrimination, thus rendering any search or seizure performed under them unreasonable, contrary to [the Charter]. In my view, a consideration of the principle's underlying rationales indicates that they do not.

First, unlike cases involving testimonial compulsion, there is no concern with unreliability. On the contrary, one of the benefits of DNA evidence is its high degree of reliability.

The second rationale [concerns] protection against the abuse of power by the state. As a majority of this Court [had earlier] indicated ... the degree to which the principle is [involved] will depend in part on the extent to which coercion was used by the state in obtaining the statements; the extent to which the relationship between the accused and the state was adversarial at the time the conscriptive evidence was obtained; and the presence or absence of an increased risk of abuses of power by the state as a result of the compulsion....

The adversarial nature of the relationship between the state and the individual and the degree of coercion in the present context are undoubtedly high.... A person has little choice but to comply with the request for blood, hair or saliva made under a valid DNA search warrant. Further, the context in which the bodily samples are taken is obviously adversarial, there being reasonable grounds to believe that the target of the warrant was a party to an offence.

However, while these factors are highly engaged, it is important to note that under the DNA warrant provisions, there are a number of safeguards in place to prevent abuse of those provisions by the state.

In particular, the prior judicial authorization, circumscribed by strict requirements of reasonable and probable grounds and stringent limits on the potential use of the collected DNA evidence, ensures that the power to obtain bodily samples is not abused. It is also important to acknowledge that, as previously noted, the degree of intrusion both physical and informational is limited....

To conclude, the [DNA] legislative scheme delineated ... is sensitive to the various interests at play. On balance, the law provides for a search and seizure of DNA materials that is reasonable. In light of the high probative value of forensic DNA analysis, the interests of the state override those of the individual. Forensic DNA analysis is capable of both identifying and eliminating suspects, a feature that seriously reduces the risk of wrongful convictions. The DNA provisions contain procedural safeguards that protect adequately the multiple interests of the suspected offender. The DNA warrant scheme therefore complies with the Charter.

YOU BE THE JUDGE

CHALLENGING THE EXPERT

The issues in the case that follows were raised in *S.A.B.* They involve not the constitutionality of the DNA warrant, but rather challenges to the DNA expert for the Crown.

THE FACTS

Matthew was charged with sexual assault and sexual exploitation of Joan, a fourteen-year-old. The charge came after Joan discovered that she was pregnant, and told her mother that Matthew had sexually assaulted her. Joan had an abortion. Her claim was reported to police, who seized fetal tissue for DNA testing.

Police then obtained a DNA warrant from a provincial judge in an *ex parte* hearing (i.e. Matthew was not informed). This was done on the basis of the investigating officer's sworn statement (*affidavit*) that Matthew was a real suspect for the offence claimed.

A blood sample was forcibly taken from Matthew and subjected to DNA analysis. Based on the test results, Matthew was brought to trial. There, he denied having sexual relations with Joan.

A key question in the trial went to the paternity of the fetus. Was it the result of Joan being impregnated by Matthew?

Frieda was qualified as an expert on DNA testing. During the trial, she stated that Matthew's blood had been subject to seven different samples, each of which had been tested in accordance with standard "international" procedures. One sample had been damaged, and accordingly was treated by testing laboratory as "inconclusive." Another sample did not produce a DNA match for a reason that Frieda described as a "mutation," an unexplained phenomenon.

However, Frieda testified, there was a match for the remaining five samples. That match compared the DNA of the fetus and that of Joan, the fourteen-year-old. Again, following international guidelines, Frieda stated that the "probability" that Matthew was not the father of the fetus to be one in ten million.

Defence counsel asked the trial judge to disregard the evidence of Frieda which was a necessary part in the proof of the Crown's case. The request of defence counsel was denied. Matthew was found guilty as charged.

In the case, there was, of course, other evidence offered by the Crown, including the fact that Matthew had lived with Joan's family for several months. And, there was the testimony of Joan, herself, as to sexual relations with Matthew.

THE ISSUE

Should the trial judge have disregarded the evidence of Frieda as a matter of law?

POINTS TO CONSIDER

- Defence counsel was given full opportunity to cross-examine Frieda both as to her credentials as an expert, and the facts upon which she relied in coming to her conclusions.
- Defence counsel did not challenge Frieda as to the nature or interpretation of the international guidelines she had described in her testimony.
- The evidence given by Frieda went to matters of fact and not law. That is, for example, was there a match between the DNA of Matthew and that of the fetus?
- How that "match" was expressed — namely, as a matter of "probability" with reference to population (one in ten million) — also is a matter of fact, and not law.
- The significance of the non-matching test sample (the "mutation") also is a conclusion of fact. Frieda had testified that, according to

international guidelines, if there had been two "mutations" (non-matching samples), her view as an expert would have been that Matthew could not have impregnated Joan.

DISCUSSION

At issue is the role of the trial judge. In *S.A.B.*, defence counsel asked the Supreme Court of Canada, as a matter of law, to declare that the trial judge was obliged to disregard the evidence of the expert because there was no foundation in fact to support the expert's conclusions.

Justice Arbour, for the Court, rejected the argument, just as it would be rejected in this "You Be the Judge" exercise. The trial judge heard evidence from the expert as to the standards for testing DNA. That evidence was subject to full cross-examination. Indeed, it was open to the defence to introduce expert witnesses of their own to counter that which was presented.

There was a reasonable basis, Justice Arbour found in *S.A.B.*, for the trial judge to be satisfied that the standards for DNA testing had been met. And, in that regard, there was a reasonable basis for the trial judge to give weight to the conclusions arrived at by the expert.

BASIS FOR TRIAL COURT DECISION
Justice Arbour stated:

> In my view, it is clear that the expert's reliance on the international guidelines

was reliance on information obtained and acted upon within the scope of [of the trial judge's] expertise. It was entirely open to the [accused] to challenge the expert on that issue. Absent such a challenge, the expert was entitled to refer to the sources within her field of expertise to explain and support her conclusions.

The record offers little information about the international guidelines referred to by the DNA expert. However, her expert evidence was tested according to the normal processes of the adversarial system. [The expert] was cross-examined by the defence, and the trial judge was satisfied that the current standards in technology and competence had been met.

It was [for] the trial judge to give the opinion of the expert the weight that he considered appropriate and there is no basis upon which this Court could interfere with his assessment of that evidence. The trial judge was [fully aware] of his obligation to weigh carefully and appropriately the evidence [given] by the DNA expert. [Further,] his verdict was not based solely on the DNA results, but also to a large degree on the circumstantial evidence and on his finding that the complainant's testimony was credible.

DIFFICULT SCIENCE

The science of DNA and DNA testing are not easy matters for judges and lawyers. Justice Ming Chin of the Supreme Court of California stated:

> The use of genetic information in court raises new evidentiary challenges. DNA evidence is often complicated and laborious to present, and those without a scientific background — including most judges and jurors — often have difficulty understanding it.
>
> A courtroom is not an ideal forum for resolving conflicts between scientific theories, yet judges will constantly be asked to referee battles among lawyers and scientific experts over the acceptance of DNA evidence. The complexity and rapid development of genetic science will [only increase] the problem. Scientists need ongoing dialogue and continuous re-examination to test their theories. In courtrooms, decisions must be made at the close of the evidence. This reality creates a natural tension between science and the law.
>
> In the United States, an organization known as the Einstein Institute for Science, Health and the Courts (EINSHAC) provides education to judges, courts, and court-related personnel in relation to a number of scientific and technical areas, including genetic evidence. According to its website:

"Our calling is to make science accessible to the instruments of justice. Our mission is to provide judges, courts and court-related personnel with knowledge tools related to criminal and civil justice proceedings involving evidence from the genetic sciences — genetics, molecular biology, biotechnology and molecular medicine — and from new discoveries and technologies in the environmental and neuro-sciences. In sum, we emphasize the science and impacts of ... technologies in judicial system proceedings."

PATERNITY TESTING/CRIME IDENTITY TESTING — DIFFERENCES

Paternity testing has traditionally used blood groups and protein markers, but these have been overtaken by the much more powerful DNA methods.

The basic procedures are the same for paternity testing as for crime investigation. The experience of paternity testing laboratories can be valuable in the criminal context. Indeed, paternity testing sometimes provides evidence in a criminal proceeding, such as that in *S.A.B.*

For example, a discrepancy between mother and child can offer information about error rates or "mutation." Many laboratories do both forensic and paternity analysis.

Nevertheless, the two applications are different in important respects. Paternity testing involves analysis of the genetic relations of child, mother, and putative father. Crime investigations usually involve the genetically simpler question of whether two DNA samples came from the same person. Mutation is a factor to be taken into account in paternity testing. It is not an issue in identity testing.

In cases brought to establish paternity for child support, inheritance, custody, and other purposes, the law gives the claims of the parties roughly equal weight and uses a civil, rather than the higher criminal, standard of proof (beyond a reasonable doubt).

FORENSIC ERRORS BY THE FBI LAB

In 2012, U.S. officials began an investigation of problems at the FBI lab after the *Washington Post* reported that flawed forensic evidence involving microscopic hair matches might have led to the convictions of hundreds of potentially innocent people. Most of those defendants never were told of the problems in their cases.

The inquiry includes 2,600 convictions and forty-five death-row cases from the 1980s and 1990s in which the FBI's hair and fibre unit reported a match to a crime scene sample before DNA testing of hair became common. The FBI had reviewed about 160 cases before it stopped, officials said.

Nearly every criminal case reviewed by the FBI and the Justice Department as part of the investigation included flawed forensic testimony from the agency, government officials said (*Washington Post*. July 30, 2014).

REFERENCES AND FURTHER READING

* Cited by the Supreme Court of Canada.

Butt, David. "How Do You Prove Murder Without a Body?" *Globe and Mail*, July 15, 2014.

Chayko, G.M., E.D. Gulliver, and D.V. Macdougall. *Forensic Evidence in Canada.* Aurora, ON: Canada Law Book, 1991.*

Cohen, Stanley A. "Search Incident to Arrest." *Criminal Law Quarterly* 32 (1989–90): 366.*

Commission on Life Sciences. *"The Evaluation of Forensic DNA Evidence."* Washington, DC, 1996.*

Dewan, Shaila K. "Watson: Scan a Palm, Find a Clue." *New York Times*, November 21, 2003.

Essig, Mark. "How Poisoners Succeed in a 'C.S.I.' Nation." *New York Times*, January 4, 2003.

Fine, Sean. "Citing New Evidence, Supreme Court Orders New Trial in Toronto Nightclub Murder." *Globe and Mail*, November 9, 2013.

Halbfinger, David M. "Police Dragnets for DNA Tests Draw Criticism." *New York Times*, January 4, 2003.

Hsu, Spenser S. "Federal Review Stalled After Finding Forensic Errors by FBI Lab Unit Spanned Two Decades." *Washington Post*, July 30, 2014.

Makin, Kirk. "Supreme Court Backs DNA Seizures by Police." *Globe and Mail*, November 1, 2003.

"Nurse Charged in Death; Says He Killed Others." *New York Times*, December 16, 2003.

Paciocco, David M. "Self-Incrimination: Removing the Coffin Nails." *McGill Law Journal* 35 (1989): 73.*

Salhany, Roger E. *The Police Manual of Arrest, Seizure & Interrogation*, 6th ed. Scarborough, ON: Carswell, 1994.*

"The Priest Whose Death Led a Nurse to Confess." *New York Times*, December 17, 2003.

CHAPTER 6

STOP! HOLDING POLICE TO ACCOUNT

Charged with an offence, standing before a court, the accused is shielded by the Charter with a presumption of innocence. Facing a police criminal investigation, there is no such shield, though how the police go about their probe will be subject to certain real conditions such as those imposed on the kind of searches that may be conducted, and the right to counsel at the time of police detention.

The job of the police is to get the facts, identify the wrongdoer, and assist the Crown in preparing charges. And, at another level, the job of the police is to "serve and protect" — to prevent crime from occurring.

Among the questions raised in this chapter are:

- May money damages be awarded if police breach the Charter?
- Do courts have "discretion" in setting a remedy for violation of the Charter?
- What differences are there between money damages in a private action and one brought for Charter breach?

The law gives a wide berth to the police in carrying out their duties. Yet, the Courts have drawn a line in the sand between what police are allowed in a crime investigation and being held accountable for improper action.

The basis for that accountability may come in part in individual actions for money damages against the alleged offending police officers. The basis for such damage actions may be based on claims that: (1) the police have breached the Charter, causing injury to another; or (2) they have been negligent in carrying out their duties, again causing injury to another.

There is, of course, also the real possibility of internal police review — sometimes with civilian participation — that can lead to disciplinary action against individual police officers. That review can be initiated both by citizen complaint and by the police themselves.

Further, should charges be pressed and should the accused claim police violation of her/his rights, a court may examine the claim and, on a finding of police negligence in its investigation, enter a remedy that could include dismissing the complaint and even an order holding the Crown responsible in money damages for the wrong done. For example, this might include payment of counsel fees for the accused, which in a complex case can amount to several hundred thousand dollars.

In two cases, we will explore the scope of each legal claim. Remember, police officers are employed by government. As long as they act within the scope of their job, it is government, itself, as the employer, who likely will be held liable for improper police activity causing injury to others.

Now, let us discuss the cases.

THE FACTS OF *CITY OF VANCOUVER V. WARD*

We begin with an innocent person caught up in a protest crowd. We will tell his story, and then move to the Supreme Court of Canada which finally decided the case — *City of Vancouver v. Ward*, 2010 *Supreme Court of Canada Cases* 27 (July 23, 2010).

This was a unanimous decision handed down by the chief justice. The fact that it was a unanimous decision and one written by the chief justice adds weight to the Court's ruling. It tends to more firmly establish the case as a precedent.

On August 1, 2002, then Prime Minister Jean Chrétien took part in a ceremony to mark the opening of a gate at the entrance to Vancouver's Chinatown. During the ceremony, the Vancouver Police Department (VPD) received a tip that an unknown individual intended to throw a pie at the prime minister — an event that had occurred elsewhere two years earlier. Neither the identity of the informant nor evidence as to his "credibility" were considered by the Supreme Court of Canada.

According to the tipster, the suspect was described as a white male, thirty to thirty-five years old, 5' 9" tall, with dark short hair, and wearing a white golf shirt or T-shirt with some red on it.

Alan Cameron Ward, a Vancouver lawyer, attended ceremony. On that day, Ward, a white male, had grey, collar-length hair, was in his mid-40s, and was wearing a grey T-shirt with some red on it. Based on his appearance, he was identified by police — mistakenly — as the would-be pie-thrower.

When the VPD officers noticed him, Ward was running and appeared, to the officers, to be avoiding them. They chased him down and handcuffed him. Ward loudly protested his detention and created a disturbance, drawing the attention of a local television camera crew. The television broadcast showed that Ward had a "very agitated look on his face," "appeared to be yelling for the benefit of the onlookers," and was "holding back" as he was being escorted down the street.

Ward was arrested for breach of the peace and taken to the police lock-up in Vancouver, which was under the partial management of provincial corrections officers. Upon his arrival, the corrections officers, following what they believed were established procedures, instructed Ward to remove all his clothes as part of a strip search.

Ward complied, but not fully. He refused to take off his underwear. The officers did not insist on complete removal of his clothes. He was never touched physically during the search.

After the search was completed, Ward was placed in a small cell where he spent several hours before being released.

While Ward was at the lockup, VPD officers impounded his car for the purpose of searching it once a search warrant had been obtained. Detectives subsequently decided that they did not have grounds to obtain the search warrant or evidence to charge Ward for attempted assault.

(To obtain a search warrant, as has been noted, police officers must show — often to a justice of the peace or a similar judicial officer — that there was probable cause to believe that a specific law had been or was about to be violated. This can be done by the investigating police officer swearing — in writing — to the facts which led her/him to the conclusion that the law noted either had been or was about to be violated. Apparently, police did not have enough information to make the required showing to a justice of the peace.)

Ward was released from the lock-up approximately four hours after he was arrested, and several hours after the prime minister had left Chinatown following the ceremony.

WARD COMES TO COURT

Ward sued. He asked the British Columbia provincial court to award him damages against individual police and correction officers, as well as the City of Vancouver and the province of British Columbia, for his arrest, detention, strip search, and car seizure. There were two bases for Ward's action:

1. *Ward sued in tort.* This is a private or individual right of action based in common law (judge-made law) principles that over the centuries has expanded — often in response to changes in society such as the advent of the automobile, the industrial

revolution and, now, a technological revolution. New facts affecting how society functions can bring what appears to be new law, though the underlying principles often remain.

There are some fundamental principles that have guided the court in the development of tort law. Broadly stated, a court looks to see if it can find that the defendant owed a definable duty to the plaintiff and whether that duty was breached in a way that caused harm to the plaintiff. And, if there were such a recognizable duty and it had been breached, then the plaintiff had a remedy by way of proving damages which, for the most part, had to relate to money compensation for real injuries. The damages were to be paid from the pocket of the defendant.

The difficulty for Ward in such an action was one of finding a duty owed by the police for what they did. After all, the police acted under orders designed to protect the safety of the public and that of public officials in carrying out their duties. The police did not arrest Ward knowing that he was not the person identified by the tipster. Nor did the police impound Ward's car knowing it was not the vehicle to be used in a confrontation with the prime minister. The harm that befell Ward was the result of an accident.

2. *Ward sued for violation of his Charter rights.* This was an action against government. The Charter of Rights and Freedoms, part of the Constitution of Canada, imposes duties on government in its relationship with citizens (and those subject to its terms). The lower courts in British Columbia found that the strip search violated Ward's Charter right to be free from unreasonable search and seizure, including impounding and examining his vehicle (section 8 of the Charter). In addition, the trial judge concluded that the city violated Ward's right "not to be arbitrarily detained or imprisoned" by keeping him in a police lockup longer than necessary (section 9 of the Charter and also, according to the trial court, a tort).

THE SUPREME COURT OF CANADA: A MATTER OF REMEDY

Ward wanted a declaration from the court that his Charter rights had been violated. However, he also wanted money damages.

(Put to the side for the moment the cost of hiring a lawyer when he, himself, was a lawyer. There is a saying that a lawyer would be a fool to represent himself/herself. For the most part, a client in a court battle needs the objectivity and knowledge that a lawyer other than himself/herself can bring to a case.)

The trial court judge ruled that Ward could seek damages for violation of his Charter rights. He pointed to section 24(1) of the Charter which provides: "Anyone whose rights or freedoms, as guaranteed by this Charter, have been infringed or denied may apply to a court of competent jurisdiction to obtain such remedy as the court considers appropriate and just in the circumstances."

The trial court judge awarded Ward five thousand dollars for the strip search and one hundred dollars for the seizure of his car. (Ward, his counsel, and lawyers for the City of Vancouver met and reached an agreement as to the costs of legal fees. So this matter was not before the Court.)

The issue was not that Ward could show actual damages such as medical injuries that might be quantified. Rather, what Ward could show was the emotional trauma incident to the police strip search and his placement in a cell for more than four hours.

The Supreme Court of Canada had to decide whether the Charter allowed for such damages and, in doing so, to state the reasoning in support of such decision.

WHO PAYS?

If damages could be assessed for breach of an individual's Charter rights, who, in the final analysis, must pay money to the victim?

It is the government (the City of Vancouver, in Ward's case) that must pay the damages. What this means, as a practical matter, is that the taxpayers who fund the government become responsible for such damages as Ward may claim. This marks a major difference between a private action against an individual for negligence and one for damages resulting from breach of a Charter right.

Chief Justice McLachlin, in *City of Vancouver v. Ward*, stated:

> The term damages conveniently describes the remedy sought in this case. However, it should always be borne in mind that these are not private law damages, but the distinct remedy of constitutional damages. As Thomas J. notes in *Dunlea v. Attorney-General*, [2000] New Zealand Court of Appeal 84, [2000] 3 *New Zealand Law Reports* 136, at para. 81, a case dealing with New Zealand's *Bill of Rights Act 1990*, an action for public law damages "is not a private law action in the nature of a tort claim for which the state is vicariously liable [where the state takes the place of an individual], but [a distinct] public law action directly against the state for which the state is primarily liable."
>
> In accordance with section 32 of the Charter, this is equally so in the Canadian constitutional context. The nature of the remedy is to require the state (or society) ... to compensate an individual for breaches of the individual's constitutional rights. An action for public law damages — including constitutional damages — lies against the state and not against individuals [as such]....
>
> Actions against individual actors should be pursued in accordance with existing causes of action [such as negligence].

EDITORIAL COMMENT

The *Globe and Mail* made the following editorial comment on *City of Vancouver v. Ward*:

> Making the state pay for serious breaches of individual rights is, on balance, a good thing for Canadians. As taxpayers they will be out-of-pocket, as in the case of a Vancouver lawyer awarded $5,000 for a wrongful strip search, an award deemed fair last Friday by the Supreme Court of Canada. But they will have all the more reason to hold police and other government agencies accountable for respecting their rights as individuals.
>
> Better to be out-of-pocket than nearly naked and vulnerable for no justifiable reason in a police station, as Alan Cameron Ward, a veteran lawyer, found himself on August 1, 2002. He was detained and carted off to jail on suspicion that he planned to pie the prime minister, Jean Chrétien. It was case of mistaken identity. The suspect was said to be 30 to 35 and wearing a T-shirt with some red in it. Mr. Ward was in his mid-40s and was wearing a T-shirt with red in it.
>
> Anyone might have been in Mr. Ward's shoes, or T-shirt, that day. Anyone might have done as he did, and made a great deal of noise when arrested, which prompted the police to charge him with breach of the peace. And anyone might have ended up, as Mr. Ward did, in his underwear. More than likely, most people would have been completely exposed. Mr. Ward refused to take off his underwear, and police did not insist.

The police were within their rights to arrest him, even mistakenly. But why did they feel a strip search (defined as forcing the a suspect to undress) was appropriate here? Was there any sign he was carrying a weapon or contraband? Was he truly dangerous? Why did a pat-down or frisk search not suffice?

The law on strip searches should have been fresh in the minds of police. It was only eight months earlier that the Supreme Court [of Canada] had ordered an end to the era of routine strip searches. As the court said in December 2001, and repeated on Friday [July 23, 2010], strip searches are inherently humiliating and degrading. Even though there was no malice on the part of the Vancouver police, they should have been aware of the minimum Charter standards, the court said.

The breach of Mr. Ward's rights could not be made up for simply by giving him back his pants. The financial reward sends the right message that some strip searches are unnecessary and harmful, and that individual rights deserve respect (*Globe and Mail,* July 27, 2010).

THE "STANDARD" FOR CHARTER RELIEF

The chief justice, speaking for a unanimous Supreme Court, made it clear that the primary interest of the Court in fixing upon a remedy was what would advance the interests of the Charter.

At one level, it would seem that the Court could have fashioned a broad remedy both as to the fact and as to the amount of damages. After all, the chief justice stated, consider the language of section

24(2) of the Charter. It allows a tribunal with authority to interpret and apply the Charter to grant appropriate and just remedies.

The chief justice, however, saw a need to structure the discretion given the Court by the Charter to set standards for application to Ward and for the future. It would be improper, she said, to cast that discretion in a "strait-jacket" to reduce this wide discretion to some sort of binding formula for general application in all cases.

SETTING STANDARDS

These are the more detailed standards the chief justice said should be applied. She wrote:

> Briefly, an appropriate and just remedy will: (1) meaningfully vindicate the rights and freedoms of the claimants; (2) employ means that are legitimate within the framework of our constitutional democracy; (3) be a judicial remedy which vindicates the right while invoking the function and powers of a court; and (4) be fair to the party against whom the order is made....
>
> Damages for breach of a claimant's Charter rights may meet these conditions. They may meaningfully vindicate the claimant's rights and freedoms. They employ a means well-recognized within our legal framework. They are appropriate to the function and powers of a court. And, depending on the circumstances and the amount awarded, they can be fair not only to the claimant whose rights were breached, but to the state which is required to pay them.... I therefore conclude that section 24(1) is broad enough to include the remedy of damages for Charter breach.

A CHOICE OF REMEDY

The chief justice wrote that money damages for Charter violation was a new remedy. It had never before been ordered — outside the common law remedy, for example, of tort (negligence): "That said, granting damages under the Charter is a new endeavour, and an approach to when damages are appropriate and just should develop incrementally [slowly, step by step, in accordance with the facts of each case]. Charter damages are only one remedy amongst others available under section 24(1), and often other section 24(1) remedies will be more responsive to the breach."

The chief justice spoke of what she called the three functional purposes of a remedy: compensation, vindication, and deterrence. She defined each purpose and those definitions will be repeated here in the language of the Court:

> Compensation has been cited by Lord Woolf Chief Justice (speaking of the *European Convention of Human Rights*) as fundamental. In most cases, it is the most prominent of the three functions that Charter damages may serve.
>
> The goal is to compensate the claimant for the loss caused by the Charter breach. The applicant should, insofar as this is possible, be placed in the same position as if his ... rights had not been infringed.... Compensation focuses on the claimant's personal loss: physical, psychological and pecuniary. To these types of loss must be added harm to the claimant's intangible interests. In the public law damages context, courts have variously recognized this harm as distress, humiliation, embarrassment, and anxiety.... Often the harm to intangible interests effected by a breach of rights will merge with psychological harm. But

a resilient claimant whose intangible interests are harmed should not be precluded from recovering damages simply because she cannot prove a substantial psychological injury.

Vindication, in the sense of affirming constitutional values, has also been recognized as a valid object of damages in many jurisdictions.... Vindication focuses on the harm the infringement causes society.... Violations of constitutionally protected rights harm not only their particular victims, but society as a whole. This is because they impair public confidence and diminish public faith in the efficacy of the [constitutional] protection.... While one may speak of vindication as underlining the seriousness of the harm done to the claimant, vindication as an object of constitutional damages focuses on the harm the Charter breach causes to the state and to society.

Deterrence of future breaches of the right has also been widely recognized as a valid object of public law damages.... Deterrence, like vindication, has a societal purpose.

Deterrence seeks to regulate government behaviour, generally, in order to achieve compliance with the Constitution. This purpose is similar to the criminal sentencing object of general deterrence, which holds that the example provided by the punishment imposed on a particular offender will dissuade potential criminals from engaging in criminal activity.

When general deterrence is factored in the determination of the sentence, the offender is punished more severely, not because he or she deserves it, but because the court decides to send a message to others who may be inclined to engage in similar criminal activity.... Similarly, deterrence as an object of Charter damages is not aimed at deterring the specific wrongdoer, but rather at influencing government behaviour in order to secure state compliance with the Charter in the future.

In most cases, all three objects will be present. Harm to the claimant will evoke the need for compensation. Vindication and deterrence will support the compensatory function and bolster the appropriateness of an award of damages.

However, the fact that the claimant has not suffered personal loss does not preclude damages where the objectives of vindication or deterrence clearly call for an award. Indeed, the view that constitutional damages are available only for pecuniary or physical loss has been widely rejected in other constitutional democracies....

In summary, damages under section 24(1) of the Charter are a unique public law remedy which may serve the objectives of: (1) compensating the claimant for loss and suffering caused by the breach; (2) vindicating the right by emphasizing its importance and the gravity of the breach; and (3) deterring state agents from committing future breaches. Achieving one or more of these objects is the first requirement for appropriate and just damages under section 24(1) of the Charter.

YOU BE THE JUDGE

NOTE REQUIRED/DAMAGES REQUESTED

The case that follows is not real. However, its essence comes from the reasoning in the principal case of *City of Vancouver v. Ward*.

THE FACTS

The City of Vancouver had experienced what it considered to be a wave of teenage crime, especially crimes of violence. The city council, with the full support of the mayor, decided to "toughen" the city's curfew law applicable to all teenagers under the age of sixteen.

A new city ordinance was enacted. It required that no person under the age of sixteen could be on any Vancouver street at night (defined as after 7:00 p.m.) without a note signed by one of his/her parents giving the youth permission. Further, such permission must state "a legitimate purpose" for the youth being away from home.

Police were specifically authorized to question any person who appeared to be under the age of sixteen at the time the curfew came into effect. The failure of the youth questioned to respond to the police officer, or failure to produce a written note satisfactory to the police, would be sufficient cause for the officer to bring the youth to a city youth detention centre. Any youth brought to such a detention centre might be identified and processed in the same manner as any youth otherwise held for detention.

John Z, fifteen, a resident of Vancouver, lived with his mother who was active politically. Municipal elections were to take place in two months. John's mother had asked him to distribute election pamphlets after he finished his homework. At 8:00 p.m., she gave him a bundle of at least one hundred election pamphlets and told him: "You are to come home no later than 10:00 p.m. — even if you haven't distributed all the pamphlets." The new youth curfew law had just come into force.

The city police chief had assigned a special unit to patrol and enforce the new curfew law. A police patrol car, clearly marked as "youth patrol," spotted John at 9:30 p.m. He had made his last delivery of the pamphlets and was about to return home. The youth patrol officers, in full uniform, stopped the boy. Politely, they asked if he had a note from a parent allowing him to be out after curfew.

John did not have such a note. He was taken to the police car, and transported to a nearby youth detention centre. There he was "processed" in the "normal" way: his pockets were emptied, and the contents placed in envelopes. He was asked to remove all of his clothing except his undershorts. Then, he was given an orange detention centre garment.

Attempts to reach his mother by phone failed for several hours. During that time, she had been frantically trying to find her son. Finally, after four hours, police were able to reach her and inform her of what had happened. Angered, she came to the detention centre and told officers the purpose of her son's task after curfew. John was then released.

John's mother, for her son and herself, brought an action to declare the extended curfew a violation of John's Charter rights. And, in addition, John and his mother asked for damages in the amount of five thousand dollars.

THE ISSUE

It should be stated what *isn't* the issue for the purpose of this exercise. The question is not whether the new curfew law violated the Charter, though we will have more to say about this in the next section dealing with points to consider. Rather, the limited question, for our purposes, is whether John and his mother could combine in a single action an attempt to rule the new law in violation of the Charter and, at the same time, ask for damages.

POINTS TO CONSIDER

- Assume that the city council had enacted the new curfew law in good faith. They really believed there was a problem of teen violence in the city and that a curfew was a way to control that violence.
- The action for damages was brought for violation of John's Charter rights.
- In *City of Vancouver v. Ward*, the Supreme Court of Canada made it clear that, under certain circumstances, a court could award damages for breach of an individual's Charter rights.
- The action for damages was not brought for enforcement of John's common law rights (such as an action could be based on negligence). The police were not negligent in stopping and arresting John. They were merely carrying out what they believed a properly enacted law required.
- The injury to John for which his mother sought damages centred on the humiliation of a strip

search which was carried out in accordance
with "normal" procedures of the youth centre.

DISCUSSION

We cannot be definitive in terms of how a court would rule
on the facts in this case. Yet, Chief Justice McLachlin made
clear some of the applicable standards in her decision in
City of Vancouver v. Ward:

1. Money damages can be ordered for breach of the
   Charter.
2. However, she stated, this is a *new kind of action.* The
   result is that the court should take an incremental
   approach (slowly, step by step). Putting it another
   way, she seemed to say that the courts should go
   slowly in defining the boundaries for money damages resulting from Charter breach. And, indeed,
   such is the thrust of this exercise.

GOING SLOWLY – BUT GOING

Chief Justice McLachlin gave an example as to when damages would not be awarded if there had been a breach of
the Charter: if awarding damages would interfere with
good governance. She cited an earlier case: *Mackin v. New
Brunswick (Minister of Finance),* [2002] 1 *Supreme Court
of Canada Reports* 405. There, it was stated that properly
enacted laws should be enforced unless they are "clearly
wrong, [made] in bad faith, or an abuse of power. The
courts will not award damages for the harm suffered as a
result of the mere enactment or application of a law that

is subsequently declared to be unconstitutional. In other words, invalidity of governmental action, without more, clearly should not be a basis for liability for harm caused by the action [of government]."

In the legal sense, both public officials and legislative bodies enjoy limited immunity against actions in civil liability [money damages] based on the fact that a legislative instrument is invalid. The chief justice stated:

> With respect to the possibility that a legislative assembly will be held liable for enacting a statute that is subsequently declared unconstitutional, R. Dussault and L. Borgeat confirmed in their *Administrative Law: A Treatise* (2nd ed. 1990), vol. 5, at p. 177, that:
>
> "In our parliamentary system of government, Parliament or a legislature of a province cannot be held liable for anything it does in exercising its legislative powers. The law is the source of duty, as much for citizens as for the Administration, and while a wrong and damaging failure to respect the law may for anyone raise a liability, it is hard to imagine that either Parliament or a legislature can as the lawmaker be held accountable for harm caused to an individual following the enactment of legislation."
>
> In theory, a plaintiff could seek compensatory and punitive damages by way of "appropriate and just" remedy under

section 24(1) of the Charter. The limited immunity given to government is specifically a means of creating a balance between the protection of constitutional rights and the need for effective government. In other words, this doctrine makes it possible to determine whether a remedy is appropriate and just in the circumstances.

Consequently, the reasons [for] the general principle of public law are also relevant in a Charter context. Thus, *the government and its representatives are required to exercise their powers in good faith and to respect the established and indisputable laws that define the constitutional rights of individuals. However, if they act in good faith and without abusing their power under prevailing law and only subsequently are their acts found to be unconstitutional, they will not be liable* [emphasis added].

Otherwise, the effectiveness and efficiency of government action would be excessively constrained. Laws must be given their full force and effect as long as they are not declared invalid. Thus it is only in the event of conduct that is clearly wrong, in bad faith or an abuse of power that damages may be awarded....

In short, although it cannot be asserted that damages may never be obtained following a declaration of unconstitutionality, it is true that, as a rule, an action for damages brought under section 24(1) of the Charter cannot be combined with an action for a declaration of invalidity based on section 52 of the Constitution Act, 1982.

CHALLENGE QUESTION

A VALID LAW?

Q. *In* City of Vancouver v. Ward, *for damages to be ordered for breach of his Charter rights, didn't Ward have the burden of proving that the law under which the police and his jailers acted was "clearly wrong"?*

Such was the position taken by the City of Vancouver. Counsel for the city argued that public officials must carry out their duties under valid statutes without fear of liability in the event that the statute is later struck down.

Chief Justice McLachlin, however, speaking for the Supreme Court of Canada, rejected the argument. She stated that the case did not involve a statute that was declared invalid. Indeed, it was not the statute itself that was called into question by Ward. Rather, it was the strip search which was condemned. This was not a subject, as such, covered by the applicable statute.

WHAT IF?

Suppose, however, that there was a law and it was one that violated the Charter. Suppose further that it was a law seen as reasonably necessary for the "good governance" of the city. Finally, suppose that an award for damages would interfere with such good governance.

Would the reasoning of the Court in *City of Vancouver v. Ward* allow for damages to be awarded? Chief Justice McLachlin left this issue open for decision. She wrote:

> Another consideration that may negate the appropriateness of section 24(1) damages is concern for effective governance.
>
> Good governance concerns may take different forms. At one extreme, it may be argued that any award of section 24(1) damages will always have a chilling effect on government conduct, and hence will impact negatively on good governance.
>
> The logical conclusion of this argument is that section 24(1) damages would never be appropriate. Clearly, this is not what the Constitution intends. Moreover, insofar as section 24(1) damages deter Charter breaches, they promote good governance.
>
> Compliance with Charter standards is a foundational principle of good governance.
>
> In some situations, however, the state may establish that an award of Charter damages would interfere with good governance such that damages should not be awarded unless the state conduct meets a minimum threshold of gravity.
>
> This was the situation in *Mackin v. New Brunswick (Minister of Finance)*, 2002 SCC 13, [2002] 1 S.C.R. 405, where the claimant sought

damages for state conduct [under] a valid statute. The Court held that the action must be struck on the ground that duly enacted laws should be enforced until declared invalid, unless the state conduct under the law was "clearly wrong, in bad faith or an abuse of power." The rule of law would be undermined if governments were deterred from enforcing the law by the possibility of future damage awards in the event the law was, at some future date, to be declared invalid. Thus, absent threshold misconduct, an action for damages under section 24(1) of the Charter cannot be combined with an action for invalidity based on section 52 of the Constitution Act, 1982.

The *Mackin* principle recognizes that the state must be afforded some immunity from liability in damages resulting from the conduct of certain functions that only the state can perform. Legislative and policy-making functions are one such area of state activity. The immunity is justified because the law does not wish to chill the exercise of policy-making discretion.

THE CASE OF THE WRONG SUSPECT

Jason George Hill, an aboriginal, was a prime police suspect in ten bank robberies in the Hamilton, Ontario, area between December 16, 1994 and January 21, 1995. The crimes, which had a number of common features (*modus operandi*), were called the "plastic bag robberies." Among these features were the methods by which the robberies were committed, and the similarities of eyewitness descriptions of the robber. These were descriptions that bore a similarity to Hill.

Police investigation turned up other evidence that pointed to Hill as the "plastic bag" robber. It consisted of the following:

- a Crime Stoppers tip;
- identification by a police officer based on a surveillance photo;
- possible sighting of Hill near the site of a robbery by a police officer;
- eyewitness evidence that the robber appeared to be an aboriginal; and
- police belief that the robberies were committed by one person.

Police released Hill's photograph to the media. They then conducted a photo lineup. It consisted of Hill and eleven similar looking Caucasian "foils." (It should be noted, however, that the "foils" chosen had features intended to give them an aboriginal appearance.)

Hill, having been investigated by police, was arrested, charged, tried, wrongfully convicted, and ultimately acquitted — after spending a total of more than twenty months in jail for a crime he did not commit.

At the time of Hill's arrest and while he was in police custody, however, there was evidence that he might not have committed the robberies:

- Two similar robberies occurred in the area while Hill was in police custody. (The difference in the *modus operandi* was the presence of the threat of a gun.)
- The police received a Crime Stoppers tip that implicated a person named "Frank" as the real robber and indicated that he was laughing because police had arrested Hill.
- The police detective investigating the last two bank robberies received information from another police officer that Frank Sotomayer could be the robber. Further

investigation disclosed that Sotomayer and Hill looked "very much alike." The photos from the first robberies seemed to "look more like Sotomayer than Hill." This information was given to the detective in charge of the investigation of the earlier bank robberies.

Because of the "new evidence," two of the charges against Hill were dropped. Police believed Sotomayer had committed those robberies. But, the rest of the charges remained.

LEGAL PROCEEDINGS AGAINST HILL

At that point, the legal proceedings began. The Crown had control of the case. At the preliminary inquiry, two charges against Hill were withdrawn by the Crown. The reason: A victim of the robberies testified that Hill was not the person who had robbed her. Later, five more charges were withdrawn by the assistant crown attorney assigned to prosecute the case. This left a single charge on which the Crown moved to prosecute. The reason: Two eyewitnesses — bank tellers — "remained steadfast in their identifications of Hill."

Hill was tried on that single count and was found guilty of robbery in March 1996. He successfully appealed the conviction on errors of law made by the trial judge. On August 6, 1997, his appeal was allowed and a new trial was ordered. Ultimately, Hill was acquitted of all charges of robbery on December 20, 1999.

Hill first became involved in the investigation of the bank robberies as a suspect in January 1995. He remained involved in various aspects of the justice system as a suspect, an accused, and a convicted person until December 1999. During this time, he was imprisoned for various periods totalling more than twenty months. (It should be noted that this was not a continuous period.)

An appeal before the Supreme Court of Canada was concerned with Hill's claim that the police investigation was negligent in a number of ways:

1. The two bank tellers who identified him, and whose evidence was central to the one charge prosecuted by the Crown, were interviewed by the police together — with a newspaper photo identifying Hill as the suspect on the desk where the identification was made.

2. The photo lineup from which the identifications were made consisted of eleven people — all Caucasians, with the exception of Hill, an aboriginal.

3. The police failed to re-investigate the cases after they received evidence that might have cleared Hill.

THE STANDARD OF CARE: THE MAJORITY DECISION

The majority in *Hill v. Hamilton-Wentworth Regional Police Services Board* ([2007] 3 *Supreme Court of Canada Reports* 129) refused to draw, as a matter of principle, lines between victims and suspects. Rather, the same flexible standard was to apply as to any claim for negligent investigations: What would a reasonable police officer do in like circumstances?

This is how Chief Justice McLachlin described that standard and, in doing so, stated her reasons. Because of their importance, we set out her comments fully:

> A number of considerations support the conclusion that the standard of care is that of a reasonable police officer in all the circumstances. First, the standard of a reasonable police officer in all the circumstances provides a *flexible overarching standard that covers all aspects of investigatory police work and appropriately reflects its realities* [emphasis added]. The particular conduct required is informed by the stage of the investigation and applicable legal considerations. At the outset of an investigation, the police may have little

more than hearsay, suspicion and a hunch. What is required is that they act as a reasonable investigating officer would in those circumstances.

Later, in laying charges, the standard is informed by the legal requirement of reasonable and probable grounds to believe the suspect is guilty; since the law requires such grounds, a police officer acting reasonably in the circumstances would insist on them. The reasonable officer standard entails no conflict between criminal standards.... Rather, it incorporates them, in the same way it incorporates an appropriate degree of judicial discretion, denies liability for minor errors or mistakes and rejects liability by hindsight. In all these ways, it reflects the realities of police work.

Second, as mentioned, the general rule is that the standard of care in negligence is that of the reasonable person in similar circumstances. In cases of professional negligence, this rule is qualified by an additional principle: Where the defendant has special skills and experience, the defendant must "live up to the standards possessed by persons of reasonable skill and experience in that calling." These principles suggest the standard of the reasonable officer in like circumstances.

Third, the common law factors relevant to determining the standard of care confirm the reasonable officer standard. These factors include: the likelihood of known or foreseeable harm, the gravity of harm, the burden or cost which would be incurred to prevent the injury, external indicators of reasonable conduct (including professional standards) and statutory standards.... These factors suggest a standard of reasonableness, not something less onerous.

There is a significant likelihood that police officers may cause harm to suspects if they investigate negligently. The gravity of the potential harm caused is serious. Suspects may be arrested or imprisoned, their livelihoods affected and their reputations irreparably damaged. The cost of preventing the injury, in comparison, is not undue. Police meet a standard of reasonableness by merely doing what a reasonable police officer would do in the same circumstances — by living up to accepted standards of professional conduct to the extent that it is reasonable to expect in given circumstances. This seems neither unduly onerous nor overly costly. It must be supposed that professional standards require police to act professionally and carefully, not just to avoid gross negligence. The statutory standards imposed by the Police Services Act, Revised Statutes of Ontario.,1990, c. P.15, although not definitive of the standard of care, are instructive.

Fourth, the nature and importance of police work reinforce a standard of the reasonable officer in similar circumstances. Police conduct has the capacity to seriously affect individuals by subjecting them to the full coercive power of the state and impacting on their repute and standing in the community. It follows that police officers should perform their duties reasonably. It has thus been recognized that police work demands that society (including the courts) impose and enforce high standards on police conduct.... This supports a reasonableness standard, judged in the context of a similarly situated officer. A more lenient standard is inconsistent with the standards that society and the law rightfully demand of police in the performance of their crucially important work.

Finally, authority supports the standard of the reasonable police officer similarly placed. The preponderance of case law dealing with professionals has applied the standard of the reasonably competent professional in like circumstances....

I conclude that the appropriate standard of care is the overarching standard of a reasonable police officer in similar circumstances. This standard should be applied in a manner that gives due recognition to the discretion inherent in police investigation. Like other professionals, police officers are entitled to exercise their discretion as they see fit, provided that they stay within the bounds of reasonableness.

The standard of care is not breached because a police officer exercises his or her discretion in a manner other than that deemed optimal by the reviewing court. A number of choices may be open to a police officer investigating a crime, all of which may fall within the range of reasonableness.

So long as discretion is exercised within this range, the standard of care is not breached. The standard is not perfection, or even the optimum, judged from the vantage of hindsight. It is that of a reasonable officer, judged in the circumstances prevailing at the time the decision was made — circumstances that may include urgency and deficiencies of information. The law of negligence does not require perfection of professionals; nor does it guarantee desired results.... Rather, it accepts that police officers, like other professionals, may make minor errors or errors in judgment which cause unfortunate results, without breaching the standard of care. The law distinguishes between unreasonable mistakes breaching the standard of care and mere "errors in judgment" which any reasonable professional might have made and, therefore, which do not breach the standard of care.

WIN THE BATTLE, LOSE THE CASE

Hill won the legal argument. He stated a claim recognized in law as a tort. However, he failed to convince the Court that the facts of his case supported his claim of police negligence in their investigation. In *Hill v. Hamilton-Wentworth Regional Police Services Board,* Chief Justice McLachlin candidly stated that the police investigation of Hill was "flawed." But that did not mean the police had acted negligently. Their actions, she said, had to be based on the standards of a reasonable police officer at the time (1995), not on what such an officer would have done in 2007.

In *City of Vancouver v. Ward,* the chief justice carried forward her reasoning relating to the need for a standard that reflects the facts of any case and, as well, a legal benchmark of *reasonableness* that, in its nature, has a certain flexibility. She wrote:

> Such concerns may find expression, as the law in this area matures, in various defences to section 24(1) claims.... If and when other concerns under the rubric of effective governance emerge, these may be expected to give rise to analogous public law defences.... Where the state establishes that section 24(1) damages raise governance concerns, it would seem a minimum threshold,

such as clear disregard for the claimant's Charter rights, may be appropriate.

Different situations may call for different thresholds, as is the case at private law. Malicious prosecution, for example, requires that malice be proven because of the highly discretionary and quasi-judicial role of prosecutors (*Miazga v. Kvello Estate,* [2009] 3 *Supreme Court of Canada Reports* 339), while negligent police investigation, which does not involve the same quasi-judicial decisions as to guilt or innocence or the evaluation of evidence according to legal standards, contemplates the lower negligence standard (*Hill v. Hamilton-Wentworth Regional Police Services Board,* [2007] 3 *Supreme Court of Canada Reports* 129).

When appropriate, private law thresholds and defences may offer guidance in determining whether section 24(1) damages would be appropriate and just. While the threshold for liability under the Charter must be distinct and autonomous from that developed under private law, the existing causes of action against state actors [such as cities, or other governmental agencies] embody a certain amount of practical wisdom concerning the type of situation in which it is or is not appropriate to make an award of damages against the state.

Similarly, it may be necessary for the court to consider the procedural requirements of alternative remedies. Procedural requirements associated with existing remedies are crafted to achieve a proper balance between public and private interests, and the underlying policy considerations of these requirements should not be negated by recourse to section 24(1) of the Charter. As stated earlier, section 24(1) operates concurrently [along with] and does not replace, the general law. These are complex matters which have not been explored on this appeal. I therefore leave the exact [boundaries] of future defences to future cases.

PRE-ARREST INVESTIGATION

Going back to the Hill case, the chief justice developed and applied the standard of reasonableness to the facts. She reviewed each of Hill's claims by weighing the facts as a standard of what should be expected of a reasonable police officer. Let's briefly review her findings:

- Hill's arrest, itself, was not challenged as negligent. The investigation, as it stood, at the time of his arrest, disclosed reasonable and probably grounds required in law.
- Hill's challenge went primarily (though not totally) to police actions before his arrest. His photo was provided by police to the media, and was published. Two witnesses were interviewed together, so that one heard what the other said. And, Hill's photo was on a desk close to where the witnesses were seated.
- As to this, the chief justice said that, viewed by 1995 standards, it was not shown that the police had acted in an unreasonable way. (The same might not be said of the standards of 2007.)
- Of more pressing concern to the Court majority in *Hill* was the claim of negligence resulting in structural bias flowing from the photo lineup where Hill was the only aboriginal. Of this, the chief justice stated:

The first question is whether this photo lineup met the standard of a reasonable officer investigating an offence in 1995. The trial judge accepted expert evidence that there were "no rules" and "a great deal of variance in practice right up to the present time" in relation to photo lineups.... These findings of fact have not been challenged. It follows that on the evidence adduced, it cannot be concluded that the photo lineup was unreasonable, judged by 1995 standards.

This said, the practice followed was not ideal. A reasonable officer today might be expected to avoid lineups using foils of a different race than the suspect to avoid both the perception of injustice and the real possibility of unfairness to suspects who are members of minority groups — concerns underlined by growing awareness of persisting problems with institutional bias against minorities in the criminal justice system, including aboriginal persons like Mr. Hill. (See, Royal Commission on Aboriginal Peoples, *Bridging the Cultural Divide: A Report on Aboriginal People and Criminal Justice in Canada* (1996).)

In any event, it was established that the lineup's racial composition did not lead to unfairness. A racially skewed lineup is structurally biased only if you can tell that the one person is non-Caucasian and assuming the suspect is the one that's standing.... Although the suspects were classified as being of a different race by the police's computer system, at least some of them appeared to have similar skin tones and similar facial features to Hill.

On this evidence, the trial judge concluded that the lineup was not in fact structurally biased. Any risk that Hill might have been unfairly chosen over the eleven foils in the photo lineup did not arise from structural bias relating to the racial makeup of the lineup but rather from the fact that Hill happened to look like the individual who actually perpetrated the robberies, Frank Sotomayer.

REINVESTIGATION

Hill's claim of police negligence in the investigation, however, went beyond pre-arrest actions. It included the failure of the police to exonerate him after they became aware of facts which should have led them to conclude that he was not the "plastic bag" bank robber. This is how the chief justice dealt with Hill's claim:

> It remains to consider Mr. Hill's complaint that the police negligently failed to reinvestigate when new information suggesting he was not the robber came to light after his arrest and incarceration.
>
> This complaint must be considered in the context of the investigation as a whole. The police took the view from the beginning that the ten robberies were the work of a single person, branded the plastic bag robber. They maintained this view and arrested Hill despite a series of tips implicating two men, "Pedro" and "Frank." Other weaknesses in the pre-charge case against Hill were the failure of a search of Hill's home to turn up evidence, and the fact that at the time of his arrest Hill had a long goatee of several weeks' growth, while the eyewitnesses to the crime described the robber as a clean-shaven man. While the police may have had reasonable and probable grounds for charging Hill, there were problems with their case.
>
> After Hill was charged and taken into custody, the robberies continued. Another officer,

Detective Millin, was put in charge of the investigation of these charges. Sotomayer emerged as a suspect. Millin went into Hill's file and became concerned that Sotomayer, not Hill, may have committed at least some of the earlier robberies.

He met with Detective Loft and discussed with him the fact that in the photographic record, the perpetrator of the December 16 robberies resembled Sotomayer more than Hill. As a result, on March 7 the charges against Hill relating to that robbery were withdrawn and Sotomayer was charged instead. Detective Millin met with Detective Loft again on April 4 and 6 to express concerns that Sotomayer and not Hill was the plastic bag bandit on the other charges. Detective Loft told Detective Millin that he would attempt to have the trial of the charges against Hill put over to permit further investigation. He never did so.

The matter remained in the hands of the Crown prosecutors and no further investigation was done. Eventually, the Crown withdrew all the charges, except one, on which Hill was convicted. Detective Loft did not intervene to prevent that charge going forward. Nor did he check the alibi that Hill supplied. Had Detective Loft conducted further investigation, it is likely the case against Hill would have collapsed. Had he re-interviewed the eyewitnesses, for example, and shown them Sotomayer's photo, it is probable that matters would have turned out otherwise; when the witnesses were eventually shown the photo of Sotomayer, they recanted their identification of Hill as the robber.

When new information emerges that could be relevant to the suspect's innocence, reasonable police conduct may require the file to be reopened and the matter reinvestigated. Depending on the nature of the evidence which later emerges, the requirements imposed by the duty to reinvestigate on the police may vary. In some cases, merely examining the evidence and determining that it is not worth acting on may be enough. In others, it may be reasonable to expect the police to do more in response to newly emerging evidence.

Reasonable prudence may require them to re-examine their prior theories of the case, to test the credibility of new evidence and to engage in further investigation provoked by the new evidence. At the same time, police investigations are not never-ending processes extending indefinitely past the point of arrest. Police officers acting reasonably may at some point close their case against a suspect and move on to other matters. *The question is always what the reasonable officer in like circumstances would have done to fulfill the duty to reinvestigate and to respond to the new evidence that emerged* [emphasis added].

THE ROLE OF THE CROWN PROSECUTOR
The chief justice continued:

> It is argued that by failing to raise the matter with the Crown and ask that they halt the case for purposes of reinvestigation, and instead allowing it to proceed to trial, Detective Loft failed to act as a reasonable officer similarly situated. It is also argued that the other defendant officers also acted unreasonably in not intervening before the

case came to trial.

The liability of the officers who assisted in the investigation is readily disposed of. It has not been established that a reasonable police officer in the position of McLaughlin, Stewart, Matthews and Hill would have intervened to halt the case. They were not in charge of the case and had only partial responsibility.

The case of Detective Loft presents more difficulty. He was in charge of the case and could have asked the Crown to postpone the case to permit reinvestigation, as favoured by Detective Millin. He considered doing so, but in the end did not intervene, with the result that the matter went to trial. Explaining his decision, he referred to the evidence of two eyewitnesses identifying Hill as the robber on the final charge.

This was not a case of tunnel-vision or blinding oneself to the facts. It falls rather in the difficult area of the exercise of discretion. Deciding whether to ask for a trial to be postponed to permit further investigation when the case is in the hands of Crown prosecutors and there appears to be credible evidence supporting the charge is not an easy matter. In hindsight, it turned out that Detective Loft made the wrong decision [emphasis added].

But his conduct must be considered in the circumstances prevailing and with the information available at the time the decision was made. At that time, awareness of the danger of wrongful convictions was less acute than it is today. There was credible evidence supporting the charge. The matter was in the hands of the Crown prosecutors, who had assumed responsibility for the file. Notwithstanding that Detective Millin favoured asking the prosecutors to delay the trial, I cannot conclude that Detective Loft's exercise of discretion in deciding not to intervene at this late stage breached the standard of a reasonable police officer similarly situated.

I therefore conclude that although Detective Loft's decision not to reinvestigate can be faulted, judged in hindsight and through the lens of today's awareness of the danger of wrongful convictions, it has not been established that Detective Loft breached the standard of a reasonable police officer similarly placed.

THE FUTURE?

Mr. Hill's lawyers — Sean Dewart and Louis Sokolov — predicted that municipalities and their insurers will begin to insist on better police training in order to head off future lawsuits. It is a frequent practice for municipalities to buy insurance against the negligence of their employees.

"This is a very good day for police accountability in Canada," Mr. Sokolov said. "The Supreme Court stated in resounding language that police are no different from the rest of us, and can be sued if they do their jobs negligently" (*Globe and Mail*, October 5, 2007)."

POLICE USE OF BODY-WORN VIDEO CAMERAS

In 2014, Toronto police announced a pilot program to provide body-worn video cameras for officers to record and improve their interactions with the public. Yet, even a body-worn video camera may need some control. For example, should an officer be able, at will, to turn the camera on or off? When should a camera be turned on? Should a court rule that the only video admissible in evidence be one where the Crown can demonstrate that it is the full video? And, finally, to what extent should police be required to demonstrate that a video was taken in the course of their duty, and not under any form of constraint on the part of the individual eventually under arrest?

A *Globe and Mail* editorial commented on the program:

> You're more likely to behave if you know you are being watched. This week, Toronto police announced a program to test what is known as body-worn video — cameras worn on officer's lapels, which record police interaction with the public. Similarly to the cameras mounted on dashboards of patrol cars and inside police stations, the idea is to protect police and public: the police against false accusations; the public against police abuse.
>
> Several other Canadian cities are already well ahead in testing the technology. In Calgary, for example, a small group of officers began wearing the cameras in 2012, and the devices are now being extended to the rest of the force. Other cities, such as Montreal, are looking into starting their own pilot programs.
>
> Toronto's decision comes after two reports suggested that the cameras could help improve transparency and accountability. If a police officer assaults a member of the public, for example, and there are no witnesses present, the wrong-doing may never come to light, or the allegation may not be believed. Absent video, the only evidence will be the testimony of the accuser and the accused, and the latter is a police officer.
>
> What little evidence we have of the impact of police body-worn video suggests that its presence

can moderate everyone's behaviour — both police and the citizens they interact with. But its main purpose is to help the public better oversee the police, not the reverse. It must be used in a way that guarantees rights and respects privacy.

People being filmed should immediately be informed, similarly to how someone placed under arrest is read their rights. People should also be able to ask that cameras be turned off in certain situations: If you invite police into your home to report burglary, they don't have to videotape their walk into your living room. At the same time, there must also be rules in place so that police do not selectively turn the video cameras on and off at opportune moments. For example, the cameras in Toronto police cars go on automatically whenever the emergency lights and siren are activated.

Video should also not be released except in the most limited circumstances — if it's material to a court case or a complaint against police. All other video, most of which will involve innocent interactions with members of the public, should remain private, and be destroyed in a timely manner. Body-worn cameras should be a tool to uphold the law, not to infringe on privacy (*Globe and Mail*, February 19, 2014).

PAST, PRESENT, FUTURE?

Police are peace officers. They have the power to detain and arrest, and to carry and use firearms. But, in a broad sense, what are the duties of police officers? In part, the answer came almost two centuries ago in the *Nine Principles of Policing* developed by British

Home Secretary Sir Robert Peel. A *Globe and Mail* editorial outlined Peel's principles:

> What are the police for? In 1829, the first modern police force was created in London by home secretary Sir Robert Peel. It is the precursor to and model for all police forces in Canada and the United States. London's Metropolitan Police Force was founded on a philosophy that came to be known as *Robert Peel's Nine Principles of Policing*. Nearly 200 years on, there is no clearer statement of what policing in a democratic society is supposed to be about.

1. To prevent crime and disorder, as an alternative to their repression by military force and severity of legal punishment.
2. To recognize always that the power of the police to fulfill their functions and duties is dependent on public approval of their existence, actions and behaviour, and on their ability to secure and maintain public respect.
3. To recognize always that to secure and maintain the respect and approval of the public means also the securing of the willing co-operation of the public in the task of securing observance of laws.
4. To recognize always that the extent to which the co-operation of the public can be secured diminishes proportionately the necessity of the use of physical force and compulsion for achieving police objectives.
5. To seek and preserve public favour, not by pandering to public opinion, but by constantly demonstrating absolutely impartial service to law, in complete independence of policy, and

without regard to the justice or injustice of the substance of individual laws, by ready offering of individual service and friendship to all members of the public without regard to their wealth or social standing, by ready exercise of courtesy and friendly good humour, and by ready offering of individual sacrifice in protecting and preserving life.

6. To use physical force only when the exercise of persuasion, advice and warning is found to be insufficient to obtain public co-operation to an extent necessary to secure observance of law or to restore order, and to use only the minimum degree of physical force which is necessary on any particular occasion for achieving a police objective.

7. To maintain at all times a relationship with the public that gives reality to the historic tradition that the police are the public and that the public are the police, the police being only members of the public who are paid to give full-time attention to duties which are incumbent on every citizen in the interests of community welfare and existence.

8. To recognize always the need for strict adherence to police-executive functions, and to refrain from even seeming to usurp the powers of the judiciary of avenging individuals or the state, and of authoritatively judging guilt and punishing the guilty.

9. To recognize always that the test of police efficiency is the absence of crime and disorder, and not the visible evidence of police action in dealing with them (*Globe and Mail*, August 15, 2014).

REFERENCES AND FURTHER READING

* Cited by the Supreme Court of Canada.

Alphonso, Caroline. "Top Court Upholds Compensation for Charter Breaches." *Globe and Mail,* July 24, 2010.

Canada, Department of Justice. *Guidelines: Compensation for Wrongfully Convicted and Imprisoned Persons.* Ottawa: Department of Justice, 1988.*

Canada, Royal Commission on Aboriginal Peoples. *Bridging the Cultural Divide: A Report on Aboriginal People and Criminal Justice in Canada.* Ottawa: Royal Commission on Aboriginal Peoples, 1996.*

Cory, Peter. *The Inquiry Regarding Thomas Sophonow: The Investigation, Prosecution and Consideration of Entitlement to Compensation.* Winnipeg: Manitoba Justice, 2001.*

Davis, K.C. *Administrative Law Treatise,* vol. 3. (1958).*

Dussault, R., and L. Borgeat. *Administrative Law: A Treatise,* 2nd ed., vol. 5 (1990).*

Federal/Provincial/Territorial Heads of Prosecutions Committee Working Group. *Report on the Prevention of Miscarriages of Justice.* Ottawa: Department of Justice, 2004.*

Garrison, Arthur. *"Law Enforcement Civil Liability under Federal Law and Attitudes on Civil Liability: A Survey of University, Municipal and State Police Officers."* *Police Studies* 18 (1995):19.*

Hall, Daniel, and others. 2003. "Suing cops and corrections officers: Officer attitudes and experiences about civil liability." *Policing: An International Journal of Police Strategies & Management* 26 (2003): 529.*

Hughes, Tom. "Police officers and civil liability: 'the ties that bind'?" *Policing: An International Journal of Police Strategies & Management* 24 (2001): 240.*

Kaufman, Fred. *The Commission on Proceedings Involving Guy Paul*

Lamer, Antonio. *The Lamer Commission of Inquiry into the Proceedings Pertaining to: Ronald Dalton, Gregory Parsons and Randy Druken: Report and Annexes.* St. John's: Government of Newfoundland and Labrador, 2006.*

MacCharles, Tonda. "6–3 Decision Called 'Groundbreaking' but Some Fear it Could Have 'Chilling Effect' on Law Enforcement." *Toronto Star,* October 5, 2007.

MacKinnon, Peter. "Costs and Compensation for the Innocent Accused." *Canadian Bar Review* 67 (1998): 489.*

Morin: Report. Toronto: Ontario Ministry of the Attorney General, 1998.*

"Officer, You're on Candid Camera." *Globe and Mail,* February 18, 2014.

"Police Can Be Sued for Sloppy Investigations, Supreme Court Rules." *Globe and Mail,* October 5, 2007.

Report of the Commission of Inquiry into Certain Aspects of the Trial and Conviction of James Driskell. Winnipeg: Manitoba Department of Justice, 2007.*

Royal Commission on the Donald Marshall, Jr., Prosecution: Findings and Recommendations. Halifax, 1989.*

The Commission on Proceedings Involving Guy Paul Morin. Toronto: Ontario Ministry of the Attorney General, 1998.*

"The Nine Commandments of Policing." *Globe and Mail,* August 15, 2014.

"Thou Shalt Not Degrade." *Globe and Mail,* July 27, 2010.

INDEX

CRIME SCENE INVESTIGATIONS

COMING AUGUST 2015 IN THE

UNDERSTANDING CANADIAN LAW SERIES:

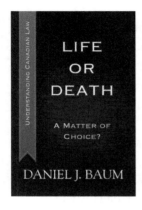

Life or Death
By Daniel J. Baum

According to the Charter of Rights and Freedoms, our bodies should be ours to control, free from state interference. But how is this principle applied in Canada? Do the terminally ill have the right to ask for assistance in dying? Can physicians insist that their patients must have certain medical treatments? Must the mentally ill do what their doctors believe is best for them or can they decide to opt out of treatment?

These are difficult ethical and legal dilemmas that we are still in process of resolving as Canadians. Right now euthanasia, for example, is still illegal in Canada, but a B.C. Supreme Court decision has recently overturned a ban on assisted suicide. Legal expert Daniel Baum examines what safeguards that the Charter offers us as Canadian citizens about our right to opt out of taking medications, accepting medical treatments, being forcibly confined because of mental illness, and asking for assistance if we or our loved ones wish to be allowed to die.

ALSO IN THE UNDERSTANDING CANADIAN LAW SERIES:

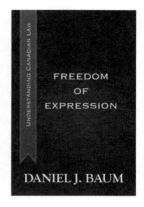

Freedom of Expression
By Daniel J. Baum

Freedom of expression is a fundamental right protected by the Charter of Rights and Freedoms, which is part of the Constitution of Canada and, as such, the highest law of the land. But it has limits. Peacefully picketing an abortion clinic, so long as patients can come and go, is a protected right, but shouting "Fire!" in a crowded theatre to cause a stampede is a criminal offence.

Tied in with issues of free speech are questions such as whether justice delayed is justice denied. If it takes years to bring a matter to court — and especially to the Supreme Court of Canada — how can it be said that there has been a fair consideration of the issues to be decided? As well, must all important constitutional questions, such as freedom of expression, be decided by the courts? Or, is there another way to resolve such issues?

How courts reach decisions in such cases is discussed in *Freedom of Expression*, an objective introduction for all readers to better understand how law and professional ethics impact those of us who would speak publicly as to issues of concern.

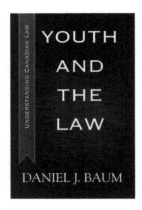

Youth and the Law
By Daniel J. Baum

Laws, as they relate to youth and youth issues, can be difficult to understand for those they are intended to serve. In the first book of the Understanding Canadian Law series, author Daniel J. Baum breaks down the Supreme Court of Canada's decisions relating to youth in plain language intended for readers of all ages.

Drawing on examples from recent Supreme Court rulings, *Youth and the Law* walks the reader through such controversial subjects as spanking, bullying, youth violence, and police in the schools. Each chapter contains prompts to encourage critical thinking.

Youth and the Law is an objective introduction for all readers to better understand how law impacts the young.

ALSO AVAILABLE
FROM DUNDURN:

The Canadian Constitution
By Adam Dodek

The Canadian Constitution makes Canada's Constitution readily accessible to readers for the first time. It includes the complete text of the Constitution Acts of 1867 and 1982 as well as a glossary of key terms, a short history of the Constitution, and a timeline of important constitutional events. *The Canadian Constitution* also explains how the Supreme Court of Canada works and describes the people and issues involved in leading constitutional cases.

Author Adam Dodek, a law professor at the University of Ottawa, provides the only index to the Canadian Constitution as well as fascinating facts about the Supreme Court and the Constitution that have never been published before. This book is a great primer for those coming to Canada's Constitution for the first time as well as a useful reference work for students and scholars.

Available at your favourite bookseller

VISIT US AT

Dundurn.com
@dundurnpress
Facebook.com/dundurnpress
Pinterest.com/dundurnpress